Mirrored Sublimation:

Essays on the Early Work of Knut Hamsun

Mirrored Sublimation:

Essays on the Early Work of Knut Hamsun

Lisa Yamasaki

Academica Press
Washington

Library of Congress Cataloging-in-Publication Data
Names: Yamasaki, Lisa (author)
Title: Mirrored sublimation : essays on the early work of knut hamsun | Yamasaki, Lisa.
Description: Washington : Academica Press, 2025. | Includes references.
Identifiers: LCCN 2025935407 | ISBN 9781680535730 (hardcover) | 9781680535747 (e-book)

All Illustrations done by Lisa Yamasaki

Acknowledgments

I am incredibly indebted to Professor Steve Mamber, Professor Eleanor Kaufman, and Professor Doug Kellner for all your advice, invaluable feedback and patience throughout the early years to now. I could never have found the depth to write this book if you had not guided me and believed in my potential, nor would I have the courage to write it.

Special and heartfelt thanks to the Scandinavian section at UCLA: Professor Tim Tangherlini, Dr. Arne Lunde, Dr. Patrick Wen, and Dr. Kimberly Ball. Thank you for your support and feedback when I first expressed my passion for Norwegian literature. Thank you for being supportive and understanding.

Many thanks to those at SASS and at the International Hamsun Conference at the Universitetet i Tromsø, notably those who encouraged me and gave me critical areas to examine. In particular, special thanks to Dr. Ingri Løkholm Ramberg, Professor Linda Nesby, Professor Lisbeth Wærp, Professor Henning Wærp, Dr. Morten Aukland, and Professor Henrik Johnsson in Østfold University College. Thank you to those reviewers and editors at *Scandinavian Studies*, *Supernatural Studies* and at *Nordlit*.

Thank you to Professor Susan Brantly, Dr. Benjamin Bigelow, Luke Beuerlein, Professor Emeritus Tom Conner, Alvhild Dvergsdal at Hamsunsenteret, Frode Lerum Boasson and John Brumo from Norwegian University of Science and Technology. All those discussions about Hamsun and Norwegian literature were immensely helpful to getting me to put his stories into the social and cultural context.

Thank you to the scholars in the early days at the Southwestern Popular Culture Conference, especially Dr. Marc Ouellette, Dr. Kenneth S. McAllister, Professor Judd Ethan Ruggill, and Dr. Kevin Moberly. Your encouragement helped me to continue writing and researching even when I did not continue with video games studies. I appreciate your belief in me.

I also appreciate and value the help of my wonderful editor, Rob Bignell, whose professional eye and supportive feedback gave me that final push to the finish line that I needed to make this project a reality.

I also wish to thank everyone at Academica Press for their work and for their consideration of my work. I am grateful for their attention.

Last, but certainly not least, I would like to thank my friends and family for your patience and understanding throughout my process of writing this book. Thank you for trusting in my intuition and my vision, as your words of encouragement have kept me on the path to further elaborate on ideas and finish my work.

Thank you to Dolores Buttry and Even Arntzen, whose work on Hamsun has been integral to the direction I took in this book. I see my work as an extension to your contribution to Hamsun studies.

Contents

Preface

Back in March 2018, I had a dream where I walked along some unrecognizable streets. A few people passed me along the streets wearing long-sleeved shirts and slacks. Their faces were unrecognizable and blurred, as they rushed by me. Unlike me, they did not smile at me or look at me the way Americans usually do even to strangers. I kept walking even though the streets were narrow, no cars in sight. Small store signs adorned the storefronts. Stores like H&M appeared, and the word "salg" was displayed in different store windows. Something told me to continue on the path, so I walked past the stores, as if I knew where I was going. Just a bit farther from that point, I reached a narrow staircase between the 7/11 and the Levi's stores. There, I saw a narrow and dark doorway.

I walked up a darkened narrow staircase that led to a slightly ajar door. I pushed it open and found a stack of newspapers almost to my height welcoming me. Taking a sharp breath, I put my hand over my head and closed my eyes to test whether I was sick with a fever, as I did feel a bit hot. When I opened my eyes, I observed that two stacks of newspapers aligned a path from the front door and led to a small barstool area, and behind that, a kitchen. I heard two male voices speaking in a foreign language. As I got closer to the kitchen, I noticed newspapers on the floor, as well as stacks of different books. I walked through the maze of books and newspapers, and their conversation became louder. One male spoke softly, while another had a bold tenor voice, not terribly deep but not high-pitched either. As I walked closer to him, he spoke a few words in English. The apartment was filled with the mid-morning sunlight seeping through the windows. I could see the dust particles in the light, a faint stale odor of old furniture enclosing us.

Distracted by the light, I didn't immediately notice two men and a woman looking at me. The elderly man stood next to an elderly woman with crinkled eyes and white hair done in a bun. A middle-aged man stood to my left, but I didn't pay too much attention to him. I sighed and didn't say a word, as I was surrounded by strangers. I looked at the tall elderly man, whose features were blurred through light. At first, he said nothing and stared at me. His eyes traveled to my lips, as if he expected me to say something.

Shortly after, the older woman led me up the stairs and into a small room. I stood at the doorway and examined the room. It had one dresser at one end of the room, my immediate left, and a window across the bed to my right. Two nightstands adorned both sides of the bed, and a small lamp was on top of the nightstand farthest from the window. Clothes were sprawled in parts of the room, as if someone were cleaning out the clothing left over from a previous tenant. The woman smiled and approached me to further inspect me. I felt myself fading as the light filled the room, encapsulating me and taking me from the scene. I resisted waking from the dream. I gasped, and the woman pulled away, as the light took me back to my world. I slowly opened my eyes and regained consciousness. I awoke to the sight of my writing desk before me. I stared at it for a minute before realizing that I was fully awake.

During 2017-2019, the bed lay across from the large window, and the light of the sun would wake me. My room was in the shape of a soft "t," in which the wider parts were in darkness, while the light filtered in through a large window at the apex. The position of my bed made me get up from the sunlight, reassuring me that I would always awaken with the sun to work on essays during the quiet mornings.

These were the early years of my investigation, when I intuitively worked on academic essays without fear of rejection and pushback due to subject matter. During these early years, I made the decision to abandon my previous research—a point that I discuss later on in this book—to start this new investigation. I mustered the courage to take Norwegian classes and dedicate my time to analyzing one man's stories and novels to find the interconnections between them. Initially, I liked one theme that the writer seemed to focus on during his early novels and a couple of short stories, but then, once I realized that his stories revealed other impactful themes, I decided to leave it and go with my intuition.

Little was I to know that the project itself would revamp and change into different versions, only to find myself going back to the original topic. As the years passed, I matured and considered how this project would realistically par with the other scholarly work done on this one author. Throughout the years, I decided to make it about the way that this intellectual pursuit changed me. While I had to edit out some of the more sensational dreams and ideas that I had written in some early drafts, I did keep some of the more personal experiences in the later drafts.

Even though the tone is academic throughout the more philosophical essays, this collection captures my experiences and thoughts. I have never been as passionate about a project before, so I am focusing on esoteric and abstract concepts like sublimation, dreams and nightmares, even though said concepts do have concrete representations. I divided this book into sections of drawings, academic essays, and essays I call academic braided, which include some academic concepts with some excerpts of the research process.

Some of the essays have been published in academic journals. Part of "Death's Symbol: The Lyktemann's Daughter" was published in *Nordlit* under the article name "Eros in the Hamsunian Male Figure: Fantasy Women in Knut Hamsun's 1890s Literature." The essay "Iselin as Object of Desire and Creative Dream in Knut Hamsun's *Pan* and *Victoria*" was published in *Scandinavian Studies* as the article "Iselin as Object of Desire in Knut Hamsun's *Pan* and *Victoria*." Since then, I went back and took out the text that I had taken from English translations of *Pan* and *Victoria* and translated the Norwegian text myself.

This book is not meant to change conversations about any topic, only express my experience of reliving some of the phenomena that I explored as I wrote my full academic essays. I will continue to explore a similar blending of illustration, reflective writing, and academic writing, as I continue to work on nineteenth century Norwegian literature.

Illustration: Knut Hamsun

Illustration: Sigbjørn Obstfelder

Illustration: Henrik Ibsen

Illustration: Opening

Introduction

Dreams as the Unifying Factor of 1890s Literature

During the late nineteenth century, styles of writing changed, as modernism slowly but surely made in-ways in Norway. Writers focused on exploring the hidden emotions within a person that often expressed themselves. In all of the stories, the writers seek to bring the previously unspoken into the light. This insight alludes to Sigmund Freud's investigation of Fredrich Wilhelm Joseph Schelling's definition of unheimlich as "*the name for everything that ought to have remained...secret and hidden but has come to light*"[1] in his well-known essay "The Uncanny." Many of the stories analyzed here do bring the previously shielded to the surface, a point that alludes to the literary trend, but also the investigation itself. This chapter details pertinent works that explain the trend and the focus on psychoanalysis as the main framework for the majority of the essays. Since most of the essays deal with the early writing of Norwegian writer Knut Hamsun, I consider it apt to open with his essay about a new form of writing that outlies his goals but also echoes the literary trend of other writers during the late nineteenth century.

In his essay, "From the Unconscious Life of the Mind," Hamsun expresses trends in the literature of the 1890s. Published in 1890, this essay reveals his confusion over how his mind worked to creatively rework stories, as well as his criticism on trends of literature. This essay helps explain a bit more of the common themes of literature in this period. Throughout the discussion of various phenomena such as dreams, the subjective experience of reality, creation of art, the importance of the sun, and sensitive emotional states, Hamsun connects these experiences in one key idea: the blurring of reality and dreams. Thus, an exploration of this indistinguishable time between dreams and reality helps infer and connect the different themes underlying all these wonderful works.

Hamsun shows his writing process as the mind's reworking of a story filtered through his own preoccupation with how others perceive his work. In his sketch about killing a hare, he writes that to kill a hare one should place tobacco next to a brick. If a hare sniffs the tobacco, it will cause him to sneeze and hit his head on the brick, thus killing it. Yet, as Hamsun examines his own writing of this story on paper, he notices a V at the beginning. After four days pass, Hamsun notices a word in a newspaper, which makes him feel a certain way and reminds him of his sketch about killing the hare. Then, upon looking at the magazine, Varden, he realizes that he did read a similar story about hunting a hare, but he had not consciously recorded it in his mind. His reasoning is that he had read *Varden* in anticipation of an attack on his writing. Since *Varden* was a Norwegian-American magazine, it was likely that Americans had criticized Hamsun's book on America, *On the Cultural Life of Modern America*. Hamsun notes that when he did read the story of the hare, he had no recollection of doing so.[2]

As he tries to understand the workings of his mind, Hamsun realizes that the mind captures some details and reworks them at night. He further explains, "I would be interested in hearing an explanation of just what it is, this bizarre activity my head engages in under cover of the dead of night, and all unbeknownst to me."[3] The words "unbeknownst to me" convey that the mind incorporates the events that Hamsun experienced some days prior to rework its recollection of events. By commenting on the way the mind takes content and shifts it only to have the writer transform it, Hamsun depicts how writing uncovers a writer's preoccupation even if it is not known on a conscious level.

Yet, if one looks at the line of harming the hare, one finds Hamsun's mind also delicately trying to save the hare from harm. When he describes how to kill the hare, he uses words to refer to the necessity of using caution and kindness in such a brutal act. Note the words "carefully," "utmost," and "gently" when he writes,

> Then you run over and carefully pick the hare up by both ears and hold it in front of the mirror, to see if it's dead, but this has to be

> done with the utmost care, so as not to cause the animal more pain than is necessary. If it seems as if there is still life in the hare you place it gently back on the grass, until it dies.[4]

An additional layer of analysis shows that if Hamsun was consciously looking for an attack on his writing, he worked his fear into his suggestion to not cause himself pain, any more than necessary. Thus, his mind also developed a defense for the opportunity that criticism might "kill" him, so readers should be careful and gentle with him. While Hamsun himself never tells the reader that he fears criticism, he starts to show how the mind develops its own trajectory. Yet, he does state that this type of phenomenon should not be confused with dreams, as dreams involve other mental states, which he never clarifies.[5]

Yet, in his discussion of the creative process, Hamsun designates this otherworldly time as a liminal period between dream and reality. Another passage centers on keen sensitivity and its effects on the creation process. He states,

> Neither dream nor reality are involved; it is a moment in time filled with a barely conscious sensation of essential connection with nature. This remarkable sensation is also known to visit people at night, in the depths of the forest; or to come to someone simply sitting by an upturned boat. There is a great deal being written at the moment about a new 'disease': the love of the sun. I believe in this new sickness too, quite literally…But this love of the sun is only another expression of the blood-deep sense of connection with all of Creation.[6]

Hamsun notes that such experiences occur in the nighttime and could involve a walk in the forest or visit someone sitting by a boat. This form of sickness, this friction between the conscious and unconscious, derives from creation, as it is part of nature to have this will apart from human consciousness. Hamsun moves away from the phenomenon of the dream itself and comments more on different experiential phenomena that people experience but do not discuss in public. He compares it to a profound love of the sun, a disease that can inflict many people, though only the sensitive find the words to articulate it. For those artistically inclined, one must accept that these interruptions of the mind occur, and such expressions in the form of strange deviations from the typical norm of the novels are indeed exemplary of the unconscious within the text. Hamsun attributes artistry to the dreamer if they have wild dreams. In saying that "neither dream nor reality"[7] exist in the unconscious, he suggests a liminal world, one that involves the mix of the mind's consciousness and the inner workings of the unconscious.

Since writers need to focus their attention on specific details of their work, they could not actively write while being in this liminal state, though some might try with the use of alcohol. Yet, through reflection of their works, a reader can find traces of this liminal space. While Hamsun clearly articulates that this phenomenon of the mind's independent reworking does not occur in dreams, as he hardly dreams, his words refer to Sigmund Freud's explanation of dreams and their role in psychoanalysis in Freud's *Interpretation of Dreams*.

In Freud's assessment of the unconscious in dreams, he articulates that the past haunts the present, as the unconscious presents the subject with previously unresolved events that manifests in the subject's dreams. Despite countering Hamsun's assessment of the mind's reworking of content as not involving dreams, Freud does define them as the mind's intellectual abilities to refute the activities from the previous day. He explains, "It is a perfectly valid psychic phenomenon, actually a wish-fulfillment; it may be enrolled in the continuity of the intelligible psychic activities of the waking state; it is built up by a highly complicated intellectual activity."[8] By giving the dream an intellectual function, it makes the mind have agency over the person, who wishes to make sense of their thoughts about their everyday interactions. By looking at its contents and our abilities to reason with certain situations in our waking life, one can explore the meanings of dreams if one only recalls what happened a day prior to the dream. Freud further explains that the dream manifests how the unconscious mixes up one's thoughts about the day, a point that shows how the dream itself is an interpretation of that one particular day.[9] In a given day, one experiences certain interactions and has thoughts of different topics, but the dream presents an insightful interpretation of that particular day's events and its meaning to the dreamer.

Initially, one might feel compelled to choose between Hamsun's assessment of the unconscious activity in the mind as not a part of dreams, yet Freud's assertion of dreams as the intellectual activity reworks the previous day's events. It could be that one dreams and sleeps without even being aware of it. As a result, in attempting to choose one over the other, one forecloses on the main point of this phenomenon. Each sample of the literature here represents characters from dreams or dreamlike settings. In some instances where characters exhibit supernatural qualities, these characters do so due because of the cultural influence inherent at the time. All of the depictions transgress certain boundaries, such as dream and reality, art and humanity, abstract thought and specific concrete object. All works discussed possess a relationship to the supernatural aspect of dreams or the dreamlike state. The representation of dreamlike characters and worlds fits in with the themes of Norwegian literature during the late nineteenth century. During this time, writers turned away from the more didactic purpose of literature earlier in the era and infused their work with more expressive tones and emotional content.

In 1905, Scandinavian writer Carl Nærup published *Illustretet Norsk Litteraturshistorie*, a book on various Norwegian writers during the late nineteenth century where he describes the main trends of literature during this time. In regard to one of Hamsun's peers, Arne Dyfest, Nærup defines the "vilkaarligeste Udtryk for de enkelte[10] [arbitrary expression of the individual]" as "Kunsts eneste og høieste Maal er Rendyrkning af stemming, Beruselse I Stemningsliv, Opløsning af alle Følelsesværdier I Stemningsnuancer,[11] [Art's only and highest goal [as] the purification of mood, intoxication in mood life, resolution of all emotional values in mood nuances]." The individual and their psychological essence permeates through "Alle Tilværelsens Herligheder: solen, havet, himlen er udstraalinger af Kunstnerens verdensrummende Hjerte,[12] [all the glories of existence: the sun, the sea, the sky are emanations of the artist's world-wide heart]." Such descriptions apply to Hamsun as to many writers who took this trend. Like Hamsun's discussion of that liminal time between consciousness and unconsciousness or dream and reality, Nærup evokes the emotions of the artist and alludes to different parts of nature from the sun to the genus of living species. Some writers fought against the naturalist trends, though adhered to its determinist assumptions. The dramatic evocation of moods coincides with an emphasis of an experience filtered through psychological means. Certainly, many of the scenes take on a realistic setting, yet the psychological nature of the experience shifts the character's mindset into that liminal place between sanity and insanity.

Such experiences mimic the space between reality and dream, as it causes one to question whether they actually experience such bizarre yet often picturesque settings and interactions with characters or if they dreamed it. In some cases, characters encounter certain settings as wondrous places but also sites of repression. Such repression turns itself into enchanting storytelling and forms of art, while other forms take away one's humanity with various forms of disastrous effects.

Freud's essay "The Uncanny" forms ideas of the uncanny from Schelling's definitions of Unheimlich and Heimlich. The uncanny involves a repressed impulse about a particular image or idea that was not originally strange yet becomes unfamiliar and spooky through the process of repression. Through repression, a person's association with a particular object or idea becomes foreign, and it takes on a different nature. For repression to occur, the person must experience a repetition of witnessing the object, person, place that will elicit uncanny feelings.[13] Hence, all the stories discussed in this small collection reflect uncanniness, a normal situation with supernatural implications. Hamsun takes liberties with the manifestations of these supernatural characters, often leading male characters to artistic production or a false sense of reality.

In Harald Næss's study of nineteenth century Scandinavian Realism, he examines the change in literature that encompassed aspects of realism but infused with more fantastic elements. While some refer to this literature as *Nyromantikken*, others refer to it as early modernism. My position is not to ascertain which category best reflects the literature; rather, I wish to show that Hamsun possessed a desire to give literature a new form by combining two different perspectives. Næss reflects on the well-known essay by James W. McFarlane, "The Whisper of the Blood: A Study of Knut Hamsun's Early Novels":

> "Hamsun also felt, like Dostoevsky, that reality and the fantastic were not opposites, rather reality contained the fantastic, and he set out to render that fantastic reality in books were unlike other Norwegian novels. Strindberg had already predicted the end of the novel and instead recommended the autobiography as the only truly realistic genre, but Hamsun combined fiction and the autobiography in a novel, in which he replaced everyday reality with 'untrodden,' trackless journeying by brain and heart, strange wandering of the nerves, the whisper of the blood, the entreaty of the bone, the whole unconscious life of the mind."[14]

In their book, *Nordic Literature of Decadence*, Pirjo Lyytikäinen, Riikka Rossi, Viola Parente-Čapková, and Mirjam Hinrikus provide samples of decadent literature and an overview of decadence in the Nordic context. Pirjo Lyytikäinen et al. explain some pertinent traits in the literature in addition to the cultural context. The literature in the 1890s shows a shift to a psychological burden as manifested by "fantasies, dreams or visions and enables the dominance of both the cerebral and—especially negative—emotions."[15] Many of the male characters displayed neurotic paranoia and restlessness and weak will, an enervated male dissatisfied with social norms.[16] At the same time, some writers displayed female characters as femme fatales and female idols[17] who did not have their own narrative. Both male and female writers of this time comment on the representation of the New Woman, a concept of the nineteenth century woman who strove for political, labor, and sexual independence.

In her essay, "Melancholy at a Crossroads: Effeminate Men in Norwegian Fin-de-siécle Literature," Kjersti Bale clarifies on the social changes occurred in Norwegian society that empowered women. Bale credits the Commerce Act of 1842 and the Marriage Act of 1888, as well as the creation of different national associations for women, as ways that Norwegian women expressed independence and gained some power.[18] Both male and female writers address this depiction of the New Woman as a female character and affirm Lyytikäinen et al.'s assessment of writers who focused on "the search for independence and female subjectivity, often intertwined with a quest for artistic expression."[19] As a form of commentary about the New Woman, the writers also addressed decadent themes by adhering to nature and its rustic power, thus showing primitivist ideals in their depiction of the setting and characters.

Lyytikäinen et al. states:

> "Moreover while Nordic decadence benefited from the cross-cultural imagination of the North as a dark place of unknown wild forces, it also developed decadent imagery of its own, peculiar to Nordic environments. Nature's potential for primitive passions and the ecstatic are essential to the decadent aesthetics of transgression in the Nietzschean, Dionysian wilderness decadence."[20]

As a result, Lyytikäinen captures the motive behind many of the male writers' tendencies to write the beautiful yet mysterious forests of the North as more alluring than society and its changing norms coinciding with technological progress. This assessment echoes the sentiments that Hamsun alludes to in his essay on the unconscious mind. It aptly sets the stage for the writers and their works in this short book. The exploration of the woman's strength manifests as dreamlike characters, artistic women, supernatural women, and their sensitive and vulnerable male counterparts whose interaction with the women changes their lives.

By indicating that the artistic avant-garde acted like an esoteric secret society, in John Bramble's *Modernism and the Occult*, he shows how literature inherently embeds some of the esoteric themes despite the author's intention. Bramble investigates the ethos of Western modernism as a longing to return to the more vibrant aspects of the past in combination with the Western and Eastern syncretism that would eradicate aspects of modernity such as imperialism.[21] Bramble defines late nineteenth century with a revival of the interest in Orientalism and incorporated these ideals into Western thought, therefore providing the interest in the occult and the exotic in the early twentieth century. Such revival of Romanticism, as seen in the fin-de-siècle, sought to account for the need to appropriate imperialist goals. Throughout the cultural and artist movement was a need to reimagine imperialism by using the symbols of the older world, thus showing a connection to the past.[22]

Since these depictions of women and man entail dreamlike descriptions, a reader assumes that these depictions in this collection include aspects of the decadent, as decadence was popular during the fin-de-siecle. Yet, I suggest otherwise. Some of the writers, such Ola Hansson, do depict the grotesquely erotic woman who lures the men, yet such portrayals leave the men in mystery as to their reasons they feel attraction to the women. Furthermore, such attraction leads men to their downfall. To best show the differences in my discussion of women in these chapters, I briefly present a discussion of the decadent supernatural woman to contrast the discussions of women in the subsequent chapters. In doing so, readers can see the differences in Hamsun's portrayal in contrast to the decadent style that was popular during the late nineteenth century.

The Decadent Woman and Her Depiction

With so much focus on the supernatural and mysterious female figure in these stories of the last decade of the nineteenth century, one gets tempted to indicate that many women depicted as supernatural convey a positive dreamlike quality that impresses the male character. Yet, it is important to distinguish such dreamlike figures from the decadent women whose sexual nature puts fear in men.

As previously stated, Swedish writer Ola Hansson, depicts the decadent woman through his collection of literary fragments "Sensitiva Amorosa." The women elicit amorous feelings yet also feelings of shame and disgust to the point where the depiction of the supernatural alludes to an ugly and evilness as opposed to creativity.

To briefly recapitulate Hansson's "Sensitive Amorosa" project, the collection of literary fragments represents men and women who experience love as a dark, confusing bewitchment rather than a feeling of inspiration. In one of Hansson's fragments, he portrays a man who falls victim to a female supernatural force. A mythical woman arises in a simple setting, a seemingly mundane setting filled with supernatural tendencies, as Hansson notes an evening in July with a feverish atmosphere. He writes, "The sun had gone down, but the clouds cast metallic reflections out over the dim plains landscape, which spread out before them in a broad view, where they had stopped at the edge of the forest."[23] The nameless man examines a woman who stands at the base of a tree. He realizes that he feels a physiological change in his brain and body, as the fever rises within him. The woman takes on the dark energy of the setting, as Hansson notes, "the evil spirit of the landscape."[24] Although Hansson depicts her with colorless eyes and seductive colorless lips, he presents her as someone who could sense in him "lust of an eternal night of love without measure."[25] The man experiences her as someone who distorts his reality akin to "dense fogs with flaring and extinguishing will-o'-the-wisps,"[26] and responds to her "mysterious sphinx-smile."[27] When he finds her again in March, he finds her eyes with "phosphorous-gleaming eyes,"[28] and her seductive smile that the nameless man eventually finds on every woman, thus showing how her energy mesmerizes him to see her face on every woman. Her essence is comparable to a lust-filled room with people engaging in an orgy. When he finally succumbs to her, he finds that the summer day's sky transforms into black filled with phosphorous shining points, or stars, forming the woman's face until these uniformly become the original woman's face that he met. Finally, at the story's conclusion, it turns out that the nameless man is standing in the middle of the street with his arms clenched as if hugging someone tightly, as people run away from him.

This fragment is the shortest of the stories in the collection, yet it possesses strong depictions of the supernatural woman who preys on the weakened man without reason and leaves him senseless. While the fragment is beautifully written with poetic phrasing and a mysterious tone that makes readers want more from this story, its negative portrayal of the woman's effect on the man leaves a reader without hope that the bewitchment led to a productive purpose. In *Nordic Literature of Decadence*, one of the contributing authors, Stefano Evangelista, defines Hansson's *Sensitiva Amorosa* as exemplary of decadent literature since this collection of vignettes shocked Swedish society. This reaction caused Hansson to relocate to Germany where he considered the literary society more receptive to his literary symbolist goals. Hansson's goal was to change from the aims of the Modern Breakthrough, which was to use literature as a means of social protest. Evangelista explains that "Sensitiva Amorosa" came to French and English readers due to female translators,

Jean de Némethy and George Egerton. Both de Néthemy and Egerton considered Hansson as the forerunner of the new literary movement as they both expressed how Hansson portrayed a "self-mythology as a seer or prophet"[29] referred to Fredrich Nietzsche's formulation of the ego and psychological complexities. When examining the terms that Evangelista uses to describe both translators' view of Hansson's work, I consider the inherent allusion to the supernatural through terms as "seer," "mythology," and "erotic mysticism." All of these terms connote the supernatural, even though only one of Hansson's vignettes portrays a man's relationship with a supernatural woman. As Lyytikäinen et al. explain, "Sensitiva Amorosa" refers to the weakness of the soul and existential anxiety brought on by technological advancement in modern cities.[30]

The depictions of this work are worthy of study for stylistic aspects in the writing as explained in the aforementioned descriptions of the themes in the literature. Hansson's depictions of women share the dreamlike qualities inherent in the late nineteenth century literature, as these women develop through dreams or induce dreamlike states. Furthermore, they possess traits of the supernatural and influence the men's emotional and mental states. Yet, I hold back from including them in this collection because my intentions for examining the women in these works differ from the category of decadent women. Despite Hamsun's good opinion of Hansson's work, his depiction of his female characters hints at their growing sexual power and strength, yet differ significantly in sentiment. While Hamsun mirrors the similar liminal quality in his depiction of the female characters, at least in the selection of his work here, he also imbues them with more complex symbolic meaning, thus leaving interpretations of their characters more open-ended than merely erotic figures.

The Direction of the Book

While many of the essays in this collection take an academic tone, they show a progression from academic to an artistic to a narrative voice to reveal the different aspects involved in literary study. Few literary analysts will take this direction, and I am certainly not suggesting that they should, only that some investigations elicit different parts of a literary analyst. In showing them as judiciously as possible, I remain faithful to the investigation. To say that dreams direct the progression of this book is an understatement, since they not only form the theme of the period in question but also dictate the subject matter of the essays as well as inform the path I took during the investigation. In doing so, I construct a collection of essays that analyze the topic of sublimation, while also engaging in it. Within dreams lies the unconscious, as I mentioned earlier in this chapter. By making dreams and dreamlike depictions subjects of study, I uncover a few details before exploring their meaning.

The supernatural qualities of the dreamlike depictions and dreamlike characters allude to the idea of the marvelous fantastic. According to Tzvetan Todorov's notion of the marvelous fantastic in *The Fantastic: A Structural Approach to a Literary Genre*, this term explains for stories that show the hesitation of accepting the supernatural aspects or attempting to use reality to explain for the supernatural. Todorov further explains that ultimately the reader accepts the supernatural aspects of the story.[31] He builds this subcategory of the fantastic from the definitions of both the fantastic and the marvelous. The fantastic is known for the hesitation within the reader between the natural aspects of the story, the supernatural elements, and a suspension of poetic and allegorical meanings of the supernatural.[32] The marvelous, however, differs in that the reader accepts the supernatural aspects of the story as an important aspect that interrupts the rational aspects, or the real-world aspects, of the story.[33] Inherent in such interpretations of the marvelous fantastic and the symbolic level of events – a distinction that Todorov differentiates – is the slight hesitation that readers might uphold both interpretations. In doing so, I perceive both the supernatural depictions but also clarify their symbolic meanings within the depictions; this aspect of the investigation coheres with the format of my writing and illustrations as well.

Since the history of the unconscious connects to the supernatural itself, the supernatural aspect of my discussion emerges within my investigation. In her study, *Ghostly Matters: Haunting and the Sociological Imagination*, Avery F. Gordon defines haunting as a part of modern social life and a point of observation and inquiry that is not a premodern superstition or a phenomenon that shows the ways one's psyche invents ghosts. Taking the postmodernist and poststructuralist ideas into perspective, Gordon discusses how those discourses affect how one might be critical of power and agency or frame one's inquiry by locating its larger context and infrastructure. Yet, she also confides that taking the ghostly matters into consideration, her inquiry allows her to expand on objective inquiry by interjecting one's experience of the matter.[34] By considering the ways that examining one's haunting is related to the subject of study, it helps to explain for the multiplicity in interpretation. Yet, since one is excavating a previously overlooked issue, the act of incorporating one's haunting in a research project implies sincerity in uncovering something previously unrevealed. Gordon states:

> The way of the ghost is haunting, and haunting is a very particular way of knowing what has happened or is happening. Being haunted draws us affectively, sometimes against our will and always a bit magically, in the structure of feeling of a reality we come to experience, not as cold knowledge, but as a transformative recognition.[35]

By associating empirical knowledge with cold objectivity and feeling with transformative experience, Gordon opens the notion that knowledge construction might entail feeling an experience with a topic or a particular subject. She examines female novelists and female subjects and uses the representation of ghosts as a tool and subject of study. Throughout her examination, she alludes to the way that ghosts as an inquiry offsets the accepted norms of academic and empirical investigation. Though she does examine works by women and proves the critical secrets in psychoanalysis, Gordon's main premise of blending the inquiry and subjects studied serves as a preface to my work. I attest to this observation though I do adhere to psychoanalysis and mainly Hamsun's writing. I examine the women within these works written at a time before World War II, the time before the questioning of metanarratives. For this reason, my investigation reveals a different motive, one that seeks to unearth new interpretations by being open to the idea of ghostly matters.

When considering the direction of the book, I also allude to discussions from Marcel Proust and Gilles Deleuze as metaphors for this investigation. A few years ago, I wrote a long-term research study that alluded to Proust's notion of memory to talk about the notions of time. In *Difference and Repetition*, Deleuze describes the narrator's reminiscence of Combray, a fictional town based on the French town Illiers. Deleuze expresses, "Combray reappears, not as it was or as it could be, but in a splendor which was never lived, like a pure past which finally reveals its double irreducibility to the two presents which it telescopes together: the present that it was, but also the present present, which it could be."[36] In this estimation, Deleuze aptly explains for the merging together of a writer's depiction and the reader's field of experiences. In certain instances, when the depiction of a character is so similar to the reader, the moments collide, as if presenting the second present moment to the reader through the reader's introspection of her particular past. In this complex idea, the depiction of a particular time in fiction becomes as real as the lived past. The possibility of this fictional past offers a person a perspective that one would not have otherwise. The layers build on more complexity once the reader tries to depict a writer's depiction as a means of literary analysis. So, I only need to imagine launching myself into an imaginary past to see if I could get closer to the truth than my own analytic lens.

I do not recall if Deleuze ever mentioned Proust's quick anecdote of the Celtic belief of souls trapped in objects. In *Swann's Way*, Proust mentions that such objects remain lost until we pass by it and "obtain possession of the object which forms their prison."[37] He then mentions how the spirit inside "tremble…call us by our name, and as soon as we have recognized them the spell is broken."[38] Suddenly I start rethinking the phrase when someone buys an antique because they felt it call out to them. Interspersed between stories of love and recollection, Proust gives powerful advice for such investigations. In connection to the Celtic belief, he then continues with memory. In response to asking us to recapture it, Proust warns us, "The past is hidden somewhere outside the realm, beyond the reach of intellect, in some material object (in the sensation which that material object will give us) of which we have no inkling. And it depends on chance whether or not we come upon this object before we ourselves must die."[39] The task then, falls on the person who decides the relevance of the object. Out of all the different forms of written work, one asks the question as to how to select this object. Perhaps this question is not accurate for this situation; the better question pertains more to one's choice in dealing with the repercussions of the selection. The object choice is easy, as one feels a particular draw towards it, a sensation extending beyond reason though necessitating reason to articulate it. Since one cannot control the pull that a story has within the person, the attraction occurs without conscious effort, eliciting the investigator's desire. Thus, this path to the past becomes a personal experience that incorporates the present moment but as a means of articulating the past.

Through my experience of ghostly matters, I examine the pattern of sublimation as it occurs in the literary works to better understand them, but I also examine the role of sublimation in my pursuit as a way to reconstruct the process of using art as ennobling affection. By alternating literary analysis with reflective academic braided essays and illustrations, I show a blended approach that encompasses the way that Hamsun's work engages my critical faculties and artistic sensibilities. While this book mainly discusses Hamsun's early writing, I do include notable other examples of sublimation from Henrik Ibsen and Sigbjørn Obstfelder as contrasts to Hamsun's representation of it. Throughout the organization of the essays, readers perceive how literature punctures through time, sometimes in the form of dreams and visions. With careful analysis, one balances the illusions to pinpoint an anticipatory event in the future or a shift in perspective. It is even possible that it one might achieve both.

Illustration: Study of Hares

Chapter 1

The Dream of the Shoes

> "Da gjorde jeg noget jeg angrer på og endmu ikke har glemt. Hendes sko faldt av foten, jeg grep den og slængte den langt bortover vandet, av glæde over at hun var nær eller av trange til a gjøre mig gjældende og minde hende om at jeg var til, —jeg vet det ikke."[40]
>
> [Then I did something I regret and haven't yet forgotten. Her shoe slipped off her foot, and I grabbed it and flung it far out over the water – whether for joy at her being so near or from some urge to assert myself and remind her of my existence, —I don't know.]

In this scene in *Pan*, Glahn sits in a boat and hurls Edvarda's shoe into a lake, an act that shows his awkward behavior in front of a woman he likes. I turn to the part of *Pan* where Glahn acts in a bizarre way to capture the attention of Edvarda—the mortal woman who contrasts to the nature spirit that I write about. This particular scene opens up the mysterious nature of human behavior in romantic pursuits, which makes me consider whether all romantic pursuits involve detective work of some kind.

After I awoke from the dream, I sit upright the morning after with a cup of coffee and jotted some notes regarding the details of the dream, as I could still experience the chaotic sensation of seizing a pair of shoes and hiding them from everyone. I turn on the light from my nightstand to write down crucial aspects of the dream before the day's events work their way into my consciousness and make me forget all of the dream, as occurs when one's obligations deter from one's deepest inquiries.

As I glanced up from my notebook, my eyes caught sight of a dark object next to my nineteenth century chair. My old Steve Madden shoes lay across from me. Their coarse leather was weathered by the years of wear and tear, but they still fit my feet. But I don't recall taking those boots out of my closet. Did I wear them after coming back from my late-night workout? My recollection of my dream is slipping past me…must stay focused.

In my dream, a group of people I had never seen before told me they were writers. These were not older writers but contemporary writers in present time Los Angeles. They gathered to play the game Mafia, which entails assigning different people in certain roles, such as such as doctor, the detective, the townspeople, and the mafia members. Usually, this process entails handing out a number of cards and indicating that the players with certain cards, such as the jack of hearts or queen of diamonds, are the doctor and detective. Players who play as mafia members are usually assigned cards of the same house, such as all players with spades. The goal of the game is to catch the mafia members through deduction of human behavior. Throughout the game, one person directs the players by giving them the cue to close their eyes and open them again. At different cues, the townspeople go to sleep (players close their eyes), and the person directing the game tells the assigned mafia members to pick a person to "kill," and later after directing the mafia players to close their eyes, the person alerts the doctor and detective to pick a person to save. When the person requests the doctor and detective to "save" someone, they cue them at different times, so no one really knows the identity of the any of the players. Usually when one plays this game, one sits in a room where the players are arranged in a circle. Much of the game involves interrogation of certain players that others wish to accuse of being the members of the mafia. Such are the rules of the game that I have witnessed in waking life. In my dream, however, the writers wished to enact the game as if acting them out would help them with their work. We were out at night at some suburban street, and we all had flashlights at our disposal.

Throughout my dream, the writers ran around and pretended to kill the townspeople by pantomiming their attacks, while those assigned townspeople also played along and fell to the ground, cushioning their fall, as if acting on stage. Stunned by the display of staged chaotic behavior, I had the role of detective, but instead of partaking in the performance, I stood watching everyone running around and falling, playfully laughing with each other. Some took ketchup to portray the blood coming from their hearts. The writers had a pact: the more dramatic they could portray the victim and mafia perpetrator, the more effective their game. It was a staged violence, without any real killing. The role of storytelling is similar to the game; the more one can convince of his or her authentic reporting of an event, the more one seizes the audience.

I stood still, and no one interacted with me. As I stepped back, I noticed the seemingly more accurate portrayal of the "killing"; as each minute passed, more players attacked each other with more force. For a moment, I thought of saving only myself.

I momentarily turned around and saw a small lake and a boat at the shore, thus breaking away from the suburban setting. The boat was still docked midway through the sand and the water. Hamsun sat inside it. I walked closer to the boat and farther away from the shouts of the other players. After noticing the light upon his head, I paid more attention to the time of the night, which I noted as dusk. The small scant light in the horizon line against a dark night sky was a backdrop to Hamsun in a small boat fit for two people, a dark indigo blue sky with bright yellow stars. He gave a smile of recognition, but before he could say anything, one of the other writers ran up to the boat with fury. This person had a sharp object in his hand and nearly reached his goal by aiming it at Hamsun's chest. Before the player could do so, however, Hamsun disappeared quickly but left his brown leather formal shoes. In response, I quickly took the shoes from the boat and tucked them in my arms; they were tie-in Oxford shoes with minimal trim and a large instep. It was an impulsive act, and the other player quickly retreated from me, leaving me alone near a boat halfway in a lake.

It was at that moment that I saved Hamsun's shoes.

When I reflect upon the strange nature of the dream, I recall Jacques Lacan's "The Seminar of the Purloined Letter," in which Lacan spends some time discussing Edgar Allen Poe's short story of a detective's explanation of how he retrieved an important stolen letter even though the French police frantically searched for it without success. The letter contains secretive communication between a member of the royal family, and D—, the thief who stole the letter, wished to extract it. Dupin, the detective, cleverly reveals that he not only retrieved the letter but also implanted a decoy of it in D—'s dwelling.

As signifiers of Hamsun's existence, I take the shoes to symbolize his identity but also the power within his writing ability. Due to the manner that scholar Stefanie von Schnurbien discusses the shoes as signifier, I can affirm that the shoes allude to a theme in Hamsun's writing. When considering the shoes as emblematic for his writing theme, I consider the idea that I am trying to catch the essence of its meaning. Throughout the dream, I asked myself, "Why am I seeing these shoes? Why are the shoes the only signifiers for Hamsun's existence?" The important aspect is that the signifier is a symbol for a meaning that helps determine the meaning of an object, yet it is also its inverse. Lacan states the inverse shows how one finds the absence of an object despite being physically present. I interpret, however, that the inverse refers to a switching of the object and the subject. In regard to the dream, the shoes as signifier refer to the subject of the person who beholds them, namely me. As the subject, the shoes refer to my ability to behold his writing.

Many scholars write about Hamsun's work, especially the work in the 1890s, delivering brilliant analyses of the political implications of his work, aesthetics, and his role as the predecessor of modernism. Yet like many other scholars, I feel the need to establish a new analysis of his work, though I seek to do so with an archaic psychoanalytic framework. The ability to see the shoes and hold onto them indicates a role I have taken. Earlier in the dream, I took the role of a detective, which is synonymous to that of the scholar. We scrutinize passages the way a detective combs through a crime scene. Despite the way that the police department carefully searched the D—'s room, only Dupin was able to recover the letter in a place where the police had not expected it. He found it in the open space in everyone's view. The letter was situated apart from the expectations from the police, thus the success in finding the letter required careful consideration of the opponent's actions.

When Lacan speaks of the difference between the Symbolic and the Real, he uses the meaning of the letter to both exemplify Poe's use of it in the story but also to detract from it. He writes:

> For it can literally (á la lettre) be said that something is not in its

> place only of what can change places—that is, of the symbolic. For the real, whatever upheaval we subject to it, is always and in every case in its place; it carries its place stuck to the sole of its shoe, there being nothing that can exile from it.[41]

Lacan uses the analogy of the shoe to refer to how the real is stuck like a sole of a shoe. In using this analogy, he indirectly refers to the role of the detective as a gumshoe, since the term itself entails the fact that the detective must walk quietly in order to be effective in her search. In this meaning, the term also exemplifies synecdoche, or the figurative term in which a part represents the whole. n this way, the term of *detective* is represented through the shoe, yet also the act of being stealthy. So, in using the detective to refer to the Real, it puts emphasis on how the real entails a search of going through the signifiers as symbols. By doing so, one confronts the symbolic level of an object. Once one uncovers the different facets of a signifier, namely the shoes, one might attain the real.

Given the significance that the role of a literary investigator is similar to that of a detective, it only makes sense that my dream refers to my role as a gumshoe. I was given the shoes in order to uncover details in Hamsun's work that have been previously minimized in other discussions. Yet, the power itself is also extrinsically linked to my ability to find meaning in his work, even if the meaning I make gathers from only looking at the symbols. I look at the symbols in order to find the real, thus departing from the tradition of Lacanian thought.

Lacan's description of symbols and their relationship in defining a person shows the power that they have in controlling not only how others perceive a person but how that person perceives herself. Inherent in this description is the idea that symbols limit self-awareness for they impede on the subject's access to the Real. Lacan states:

> Symbols in fact envelop the life of man with a network so total that they join together those who are going to engender him 'by bone and flesh' before he comes into the world; so total that they bring to his birth, along with the gift of the stars, if not with the gift of the fairies, the shape of his destiny; so total that they provide the words that will make him faithful or renegade, the law

> of the acts that will follow him right to the very place where he is not yet and beyond his very death.[42]

Lacan's allusion to supernatural aspects aptly describes the relevance of the supernatural. The symbols indeed convey a power to determine one's fate, such as the way that a person uses the stars to guide their future or the way by which a protagonist tries to please the fairies in the fairytales. By investigating these symbols, especially the supernatural as alluded to in the "fairies" and "stars," I examine how they inform an understanding of Hamsun's work. The investigation into the supernatural makes us look at Hamsun's use of symbols as beyond the Symbolist trends in literature at the time. In so far as the words "make him faithful or renegade," a reader sees consistency in the use of the symbols, in particular, the different components of the dream. As for the role of detective in the dream, it is the only detail that is consistent to my daily life.

The dream depicted a game that people performed, yet it was the vivid details in the acting that I recalled. In particular, the anger that one writer had to stab Hamsun is understandable given Hamsun's political choices and shortcomings. A number of scholars expound on their criticism of his politics and personal biases such as his bias against women's liberation, the indigenous Sami, the integration of African-Americans into American society, and his ill treatment of Jewish people in his travel stories. All their criticism is justly articulated and rightfully elaborated on. In 2023, Norwegian scholars, in particular Ståle Dingstad, Lisbeth Wærp, and Henning Wærp, debated on whether one should discuss and write about Hamsun and his work arose in 2023; the verdict stood that writers may do so but consider the ethical responsibility in addressing aesthetics in Hamsun's work.

In her book, *Knut Hamsun: The Dark Side of Literary Brilliance*, Monika Žagar aptly summarizes the themes of Hamsun's literature as "the return to the idealized land, the return to traditional gender roles, the acceptance of one's social role, and ignorance of politics" and the way they coincide with "the ideological propaganda of National Socialist parties."[43] In Hamsun's depiction of the Sami, he relegates their culture and connection to nature as flat characters in his work.[44] In Žagar's assessment of Hamsun's treatment of mixed-race and exotic women, she examines *Segelfloss Town* and *Livets Spil* as examples where the exotic women are either given retribution for their choices or offered the choice of assimilation. In her assessment of Segelfloss Town, Žagar writes how the bright and beautiful mixed-race woman chooses marriage with a Norwegian man and chooses to only speak Norwegian. Žagar indicates that this depiction "celebrate[s] the victory of the dominant white culture as it either fully assimilated the foreign or accepted only token differences."[45]

Such assessment mirrors James W. McFarlane's critique of Hamsun's treatment of women. McFarlane closes his article, "The Whisper in the Blood: Hamsun's Early Novels," with an assessment of Hamsun's cruel opinion of women: "He claimed that woman is inferior to man, physically and intellectually, and that she is therefore driven to exercise a tyranny over him by unworthy methods."[46] In other words, Hamsun's ideas and political biases ensured anger from readers. While his literature vividly portrays the sensitivity of an artist as well as the unconscious of one's desires, it does not take away from the cruelty in his biases and in his later political alliance with the Nazi party.

In his article "Prophet of Regeneration: On Two Fascist Readings of Knut Hamsun," Dean Krouk examines two studies on fascist thought in order to show Hamsun's fascist tendencies. A consistent theme in Hamsun's writing is a "mythical use of a vanished or imagined past to construct a political alternative to liberal modernity."[47] While many authors refer to the mythical past, Krouk aptly gives a distinction that in fascist thought the imagined past is perceived as the key to eradicate any liberties that accompany progressive societies. As Krouk indicates in his use of Roger Griffin's definition, fascism entails a particular "national or ethnic cleansing."[48] Since my study examines the supernatural and mythical in fin de siècle Norwegian literature, I am careful not to celebrate Hamsun's novelty in expressing a new age and life as a way to support his fascist thought. Rather, I examine the way that the supernatural characters comment on certain tendencies that Hamsun might not be aware of on a conscious level, such as his depiction of supernatural women who possess power over the male protagonist. The way by which the male characters incorporate their creative energy into their identities suggests that Hamsun considered women powerful but feared them due to it. I also do not exonerate him from his prejudices, as he lacked the insight of seeing value in different races and an open mind in perceiving the equality between men and women. By exploring a theme in some of his early work, I consider a theme that he did not openly address and hint that through his inability to confront his emotions, part of his mind betrayed him.

Insofar as Hamsun's early work helped to show how social norms control much of human behavior as seen in the how the characters step outside of convention,[49] it was revolutionary in literature to depict humans as fractured. Through the unleashing of their repressions, characters could confront deeper fears, desires, and frustrations. Some confrontations with one's deepest emotions make the person experience the emotions more intensely, particularly if the person has not previously admitted such emotions to themselves. In this respect, the person experiencing such emotions would consider them amplified—as if it is beyond human capacity. For this reason, the representation of the supernatural takes precedence over other interpretations of the work.

Referring back to my dream, I consider the issue of the shoes and the strange behavior from the other writer when I found Hamsun in the boat. Enacting the role of the mafia game, the other writer wanted the power in the shoes, but didn't want the shoes themselves…or I took the shoes faster than he could take them.

In *Pan* when Hamsun states Glahn's motivation for throwing Edvarda's shoe in the water, he wishes to assert his existence, to remind her of him. His act symbolizes a willingness to show his existence, or at least prove it to her. He becomes aware that he does exist, and he wishes to show this same consciousness to her. In regard to my dream, the shoes signified of Hamsun's rigor in his writing. Since the shoes manifested Hamsun's writing ability or aesthetic in his writing, they acted as a part of his existence that the writer wanted, as in the fame in powerful writing.

The sunlight has made its way into my room, removing all traces of that early morning when darkness still fills the room with last night's wishes. Was the dream a clue to my investigation? Why did it feel more like a part of my existence than an actual dream? Perhaps the essay on sublimation is making me preoccupied with the idea. After all, I do wish to convey my ideas clearly. I am excited about the upcoming gathering where I do get a chance to report my analysis on the literature.

I go to my desk and pull out a sheet of paper to capture the shoes. Using different forms of lead pencils to layer lines of darkness on the page, I emphasize the creases and the bruises on the shoes. The different traces of dirt permanently discolored them after I neglected to clean them after particular moments of wear. In my drawing, I position the shoes so that the viewer cannot look at anything else but these shoes. Their gaze would remain on the misshaped form of the leather and the different length of laces. Such details further accentuate from my firm grip on the pencils.

Due to the fact that I never wanted to give them up or throw them out, I kept them a despite their worn-down condition. One might say that I kept them around to remind me of the days when I would go out in the middle of the night and find myself looking into bathroom mirrors where I realized that my gaze looked differently than I remembered. Or perhaps it is just my recollection of my younger years when I was at an age of abundant creativity, a time when one cared about the passing of time, as one was always ensured that they had enough of it.

Once I was able to properly examine the shoes through rendering it, I could see how the laces constrained the form. They were worn and discolored in the toe area and misshaped from years of wear. The leather was thin and vulnerable to weather. One shoe buckled in the back, while the other was a bit firmer and held onto its shape. Both shoes, though, lost their shape during the years of different transitions in dressing style. I don't wear them as much as I used to. And now, they are standing in for some shoes that I am drawing for the sake of an experiment. Since they are the only pair that remind me of old boots that someone from the past would wear, I am using them as models for shoes that Iselin might have worn. Yet, I am attempting to capture not so much "Iselin's shoes," but more so the abstract quality of upholding a part of the past without making it about the shoes itself.

While the shoes do stand in for the time of remembrance of one's young life filled with affection, they stop becoming what they once were for me. I don't wear them but instead, consider them as a visual cue to continue this experiment. Even if no academic has tried this approach before, it is worth doing so to uncover what might occur, as one art form inspires another. This sort of detective work does not entail putting together all the clues to generate a solution to the overall puzzle, but rather, how a part of a story engenders art in another form yet only through the process of literary investigation. In short, I am taking experimental humanities in a new direction without developing a new technology, except for the possibility of following the "signifying chain" up to a certain point.

Eventually I do buy new boots that have fabric on the sides extending up past the ankle, so they no longer constrict my ankles when I walk around. These boots don't have a heel and make walking around more comfortable. Months later, after I finish drawing the older boots, I do not find them anywhere when going through my closet. I recall making a mental note to give them away to a second-hand store, but I myself do not do so. At least, I do not remember doing so.

Illustration: Study of Boots

Chapter 2

Iselin as Object of Desire and Creative Dream in Hamsun's novels *Pan* and *Victoria*

Knut Hamsun's novels *Pan* and *Victoria* focus on the tragedies of the attainment of love and then, its subsequent loss due to the pressures of social conventions and responsibilities. In *Pan*, the male protagonist, Thomas Glahn, meets Edvarda, the daughter of a wealthy merchant, and attempts to consummate his love for her. Due to an inability to engage in social interactions as he relates more to nature, Glahn cannot properly continue his relationship with Edvarda. In *Victoria*, Hamsun writes of Johannes Møller, the son of a miller, who falls in love with the daughter of a landowner, Victoria. She returns his love but cannot show him his love due to her familial responsibilities. While many scholars focus on the Glahn's and Johannes's respective troubled relationships with the mortal women, they only discuss Iselin, a nature spirit, in respect to Glahn's relationship with nature and his ideal of a feminine woman.

In *Pan*, Hamsun initially introduces Iselin as an amorous nature spirit, a legend that comes alive when the protagonist enters the northern forest. In Even Arntzen's article, "Munken Vendt—på sporet av Knut Hamsuns mytiske estetikk," he considers the characters fantasy characters that arise from Glahns's mind.[50] Once again, in *Victoria*, Iselin appears as a character from one of Johannes's fictional writings. Johannes creates Munken Vendt, as his poetic voice, and through the narration of Munken Vendt, a reader finds Iselin.[51] While I do not discuss Iselin in greater detail in Hamsun's later drama, *Munken Vendt*, I will mention that Hamsun develops her ethereal character into a mortal woman, who also loves Munken Vendt, yet does not overcome his initial rejection of her. Though I do not discuss the difference of interpretations in context of the play, I broach this difference in perspective of Iselin to refer to Hamsun's formulation of Iselin's character. For some readers, Iselin remains mythical and symbolic of a mythical female figure of creation, a point that supports my view of Iselin as the origin of sublimated desire. In this article, I use Jacques Lacan's ideas on sublimation to describe four different aspects of how Iselin evokes libidinal desire from the male characters. The first part entails Glahn's encounter with Iselin as a nature deity in *Pan*, as an understanding of her as a beautiful yet disarming creature. Then, I show how Iselin's beauty inspires the male characters to take up some of her characteristics, and finally how the male characters channel Iselin through storytelling and writing. In my discussion of the first few steps, I explain Iselin's role as she appears in *Pan*, then I discuss Iselin in *Victoria* and *Pan* in the latter steps.

Though her role is less significant in *Victoria* than in *Pan*, Iselin alludes to mystical creativity, a manifestation of feminine energy manifested through male fantasy. By evoking libidinal impulses within the male protagonists, they experience sexual feelings for a nature spirit but sublimate this energy in order to create art through stories. Through an investigation of Lacan's ideas of sublimation, I consider the relationship that Hamsun's male characters have with Iselin, as a deity, and object of desire that inspires proliferation of writing instead of a desire to eradicate the impulse. In my examination, I demonstrate Iselin's presence as paramount to the novels' expression of love and desire. My discussion of both novels reveals a progression of how Iselin is idolized, mainly through the events in *Pan*, and then sublimated as seen in both *Pan* and *Victoria*.

Nature and Vitalism

Hamsun's emphasis on nature is not a new insight, as many scholars continue to address it in their work. In Monika Žagar's book, *The Dark Side of Literary Brilliance,* she aptly explains the Norwegian cultural background during the nineteenth century as involving a conflict between modernism as seen in the crowded urban cities, use of newer forms of technological advancements, and the Norwegian focus on nature as the primitive ideal. As part of the earlier preoccupation with finding a Norwegian identity after their independence from Denmark, Norwegians focused on constructing identities of cultivated people with access to their primitive side. Norway became known as a site of natural rebirth for artists, who used their natural environment to distinguish their voices from others and captivate their readers.[52] Offering a similar perspective, Arne Lunde explicates that Hamsun's male figures, most relevant in this case Johannes and Glahn, symbolize the struggle between nature and modernization. Such "soulful wander-artists" depict the way that Hamsun clashes with the conformist reality. Their fantasies as depicted in writing and thoughts are reactions against modern ideals such as democracy, urbanization and conformity.[53]

When discussing *Pan* as part of the fin de siècle literature that exposes ennui as opposed to aesthetics for the artistic restless behavior, Pål Bjørby describes Hamsun's novel as a return to nature. Aptly connecting the pattern between the women and nature, Bjørby states, "Hamsun describes exhaustion, anxiety, and nervousness in a destabilized bourgeois male self, who is uncertain about how to live in a modern world and whose effort to salvage the self requires a return to nature…The restoring of the self includes…a return to uncluttered desire, sex, and Woman."[54] An underlying connection in Bjørby's observations of nature, art, and male desire for women is one on identity and the way that the self involves an association among nature, desire for women, and art.

When looking into the theme of the occult in Western history, Antoine Faivre delineates four characteristics in the esoteric aspects in Modernism. They include the following: 1. The idea of correspondence, the idea that explains the parallel nature between the outer planets and the human; 2. Nature as a living entity that binds the human to the divine; 3. The role of rituals in the symbolic transaction between the human and the divine; and 4. The transformation of oneself as a another being, and often times involving a transmission of one stage to the next.[55]

The focus on nature relates to Frode Lerum Boasson's assertion of the vitalistic impulse that Hamsun's male characters honor as seen in particular in their return to nature after having failed social interactions. Hamsun's expression of man's natural impulse refers to his goal in literature to uncover the mimosa sensibilities, or the acute sensitivities that the mimosa plant experiences upon touch.[56] Moreover, Hamsun's use of the Greek mythological figure, Pan, in the eponymous work, *Pan*, demonstrates his belief that modern technology displaces art and natural life.[57] Boasson further explains that *Pan* symbolically addresses the notion of vitalism, or the attempt to return to life after its decay. When he mentions that Hamsun attempts to bring back life after its decay in modernism, he describes vitalism as an unconscious force throughout nature that only certain humans can access.[58] As I consider one of his explanations of the mimosa impulse as a depiction of the vitalistic force, I consider my discussion of the libidinal impulse as exemplary of a type of vitalism, one that enables male characters to create stories.

Iselin and Sublimation

In his lecture series on *Ethics in Psychoanalysis*, Lacan initially contributes to Freud's notion of sublimation, which Freud defines as "a process that concerns object-libido and consists in the instinct's directing itself towards an aim other than, and remote from, that of sexual satisfaction."[59] Although other accounts of Freudian sublimation reveal it to be some form of repression, substitute desexualized symptoms, and a defense against repression,[60] a more important defining factor of sublimation is its connection to repression. Despite a lack of complete clarity on the origin of sublimation and its relation to repression, early conceptions incorporate a turning away of the object-libido into the self.[61] Providing a different view of sublimation, Lacan states that satiation of desire involves a reading of desire as a chain of metaphors and metonyms. He further comments, "the properly metonymic relations between one signifier and another that we call desire is not a new object or a previous object, the change of the object itself."[62] Lacan incorporates Freud's further development of sublimation as a desexualized energy that makes the subject abandon feelings for the object and internalize it as part of the ego[63] when Lacan formulates the example of courtly love.

By examining the function of courtly love poetry, Lacan illustrates that humans want an object that is idealized to the point of not being real. When the poet reframes the woman as a symbol and metaphorically refers to the symbol itself in lieu of the woman, he explicitly alludes to her in a sexual way. By doing so, the poet constructs the object of desire as unattainable and necessitating multiple barriers in order to increase the feeling of desire. Even in terms of her qualities, she is glorified beyond human measures, thus stripping her of her human abilities. Essentially, the subject falls for the impossible or the unreal, the void that Lacan refers to as "the vacuoule."[64] This concept touches upon the process in sublimation in which the subject aggrandizes an object to the level of The Thing—a "beyond of the sacred" element,[65] possibly alluding to a sublime essence to which one attributes powers of a deity. Human beings have desired for objects based on its associations with *Das Ding* (The Thing), but they do not have access to the Thing-in-itself.

When Lacan discusses the Das Ding as a primordial object that originates desire, he posits that it is comprised of different parts that signify different meanings in addition to being an object "refound" and never truly lost. The vase is a dualistic object that creates a void only to fill it and represents the notion of Das Ding, a void in which one fills yet also that which creates the same object to be filled.[66] Both previous descriptions of the vase exemplify the idealization of Iselin as a mythological creature, as the origin of an ideal for other women yet also that which the male protagonists use to judge the other women, thus creating a void in their response to these other women.

While not specifically commenting on Iselin's character in *Hele Livet en Vandrer i Naturen,* Henning Howlid Wærp mentions Glahn's sympathy toward nature arises as an experience that eradicates the division of Glahn as a perceiving subject and nature as the object being perceived.[67] In other words, a reader might consider Wærp's assessment of the narrative shift in *Pan* as a way to explain for Iselin's creation as a character. Since she is part of the forest and comes alive only when Glahn comes to the forest, her character only speaks and interacts with Glahn due to the fact that he is so immersed with her.

When Hamsun first mentions Iselin in *Pan,* he does so through Glahn's solace of solitude and the forest, thus associating her with a mythological forest spirit. The time is one o'clock in full spring when birds are alive and the sun descends for a short while before rising once more. Hamsun imbues her with nature in the repeated line that acts as a simultaneous description of the early morning sun descending into the sea: "Men solen dukker skiven ned i havet og kommer så op igjen, rød, fornyet, som om den har været nede og drukket"[68] ["But the sun dips its disk into the sea and then comes up again, red, renewed, as if it has been down and drunk"]. This same line occurs an hour after Glahn has consummated his love with Iselin. His experience with her shows playful restraint on her part, as depicted after their hour together when she utters words against his mouth.

Through Glahn's experience with her, readers perceive Iselin as a nature spirit, a manifestation of love for the forest. Iselin's breath is more like "en iling [at] går gjennom skogen"[69] ["A rush (that) sweeps through the forest"]. Glahn notes Iselin's presence "pusler i græsset"[70] ["rustles in the grass"] as if they could be "løv som faldt til jorden…også være trin"[71] ["leaves that fell to the ground…also (could)be footsteps"]. Then, Glahn fantasizes about Iselin as a prayer to different hunters, an existence in these woods from four generations ago. Her voice is akin to "syvstjærnen synger gjennem mit blod"[72] ["the seven-star (the Pleiades) singing in his blood"], a quality that aligns with heavenly features. After the encounter, Hamsun describes Iselin as having a face tender and rapturous as she waves goodbye to Glahn. Affirming Hamsun's sensuous description of Iselin, Dolores Buttry refers to her as an "embodiment of eros"[73] in Buttry's examination of Iselin's character in *Pan* and in *Munken Vendt.* Arntzen attributes Glahn's accessibility to Iselin's presence to the legend where she came from.[74] Inherent in Arntzen's description of Iselin as a legend, Iselin's character as a higher essence establishes her as a higher deity.

By giving Iselin attributes of the beautiful yet mysterious nature spirit, Hamsun imbues Iselin with a beauty that simultaneous lures lovers but also ironically drives them away. Insofar as Iselin has different lovers, she visits them at different occasions, thus alluding to periods of time without satisfaction. In relation to Lacanian desire, the point of desire is not to satiate it but to maintain the feeling of desire and change not only the men who desire but the men's relation to Iselin. Lacan expresses the function of the beautiful in relation to desire. Artists experience dissatisfaction as they capture the Beautiful, since in doing so, they confront the idea that the Beautiful disarms desire, thus separating them from the Beautiful. When Lacan defines the Beautiful as "suspending, lowering, disarming desire"[75] yet eliciting a form of desire that arises in a rupture between pain and pleasure, he affirms that the quest for a beautiful object, be it a person or an ideal, incorporates conflicted feelings. Lacan mentions that the subject vanishes and alienates himself through the process of expressing desire to an object. The subject becomes a series of signifiers by appealing to the object as need.[76] Furthermore, Lacan mentions that the idealized woman is a mirrored image of the artist's quest to seek her.[77] The artist matches the traits of the object of desire to his ideal; since it involves some of the artist's identity, it alludes to a narcissist function. If the woman has ideal aspects inherent in the social norms one comes from, she is a projected view of the subject's ego ideal, thus mirroring the intrapersonal split Freud suggests within the ego and id.

In the essay, "Field and Function of Speech and Language in Psychoanalysis," Lacan explains how desire causes the object disappear and reappear in the guise of what the subject's alter ego, or ego ideal, wishes it to be. Though Lacan addresses the Fort Da! game that Freud's grandson played, he means to offer this anecdote as an explanation for what occurs when the subject uses words from his language to locate and name an object of desire. As in the Freudian anecdote of the boy's game of using a wooden spool to symbolize the disappearance and reappearance of his caretaker, the subject also enters a similar field of signifiers when making sense of the object of desire. The difference between desire and need also obscures the way by which the subject understands his desire.[78] The identity of the object diminishes, as the subject makes sense of her through his pursuit of desire.

The quest for the Beautiful also relates to the role of the artist or poet in so far as they lure their audience to experience multiple emotions by using different signifiers. Some examples of such signifiers include objects such as the parasols, hats, hands, shoes, and eyes as partial objects, or objects that Stefanie von Schnurbein refers to as fetishistic objects.[79] While such signifiers refer to Glahn's focus on mortal women, he starts noting their distinctive features as a reaction to his experience of desire from Iselin. The partial objects, in this case, different aspects of the female characters, refer to the function of Das Ding. Aspects such as Iselin's voice, shoes, animalistic gaze, and amorous disposition make Glahn idealize her as a humanlike embodiment of nature's fecundity in summer.

Hamsun presents examples of the focus on shoes occur in the erotic moments. In the forest as she gets intimate with Glahn, she playfully tells him and repeats her line “Å du binder ikke mit skobånd, du min kjæreste, nei du binder ikke…binder ikke mit…”[80] [“you are not tying my shoelaces, you my love, no you do not tie, tie not my…”] and leaves her sentence unuttered. This detail suggests that she and Glahn bond intimately as the sensation leaves her unable to speak. These focus on her shoelaces suggest that like her untied laces, she is also becoming undone.

In a similar manner, Hamsun depicts a bit of fear in Iselin’s narrative because she mentions her fear of making noise three times in her initial narrative of being with Dundas: “Jeg var rædd for at han skulde høre det...Jeg var så rædd for støien av hans store støvler…Jeg var også så rædd for den knakende”[81] [“I was afraid that he should hear it…I was so afraid for the noise of his big boots…I was also so afraid for the cracking one”]. This mix of anticipation and fear of alerting others to her night of passion refers to her playful restraint in her night with Glahn. Her fear of the sound of the crackling his heavy boots would alarm her maid, which Iselin does not desire. This element of secrecy in her act goes away once Dundas makes noise with his boots. Just like her own admission of how Glahn did not tie her laces during intimacy, Iselin notes the heavy sound of boots. Yet, his fixation of Iselin’s erotic essence allows him to incorporate Iselin’s actions into his personality, such as her ability to have different lovers.

As Iselin herself becomes synonymous with having multiple lovers, in this respect, collecting different lovers, it inspires Glahn to make the necessary sacrifices that might incur more desire. When Glahn leaves a party because he hears nature, like the sound of birds, he leaves at 1 a.m., showing how the different sounds of nature and time are signifiers for Iselin. When Glahn chooses nature over Edvarda, he actuates the similar actions that Iselin does, foregoing one lover for another.[82] Furthermore, Glahn shows this duplicity when he addresses his different loves to Eva. During his Iron nights, a time in late summer when the night’s cool temperature kills the summer’s blooms, Glahn spends three nights in the forest, marking a narrative shift in the story. In his immersion with the forest, he comes to the realization of his identity and connection with nature. During his Iron nights in the forest, Glahn discovers his main conflict and purpose of his subjectivity: "Jeg elsker en kjærlighetsdrøm jeg hadde engang, jeg elsker dig og jeg elsker denne plet jord"[83] ["I love a dream of love I once had, I love you, and I love this patch of land"]. The Norwegian word "kjærlighetsdrøm" depicts the dream as a love dream as opposed to a general dream, thus referring to Glahn's dream of love for Iselin, and by extension, the forest. In return, Glahn channels his love for Iselin into his writing. Since Glahn addresses Eva, one of his lovers, he notes that he does love her, but he loves the intensity that she shows him, rather than the person she is. This intensity Eva bestows upon him is similar to the devotion he shows to Iselin, and by extension to nature.

Like Iselin, Glahn is also described as having intense eyes. Initially describing Iselin as giving him a sign of her infatuation for Glahn, he indicates "Hun vil gi mig et vink med øinene å forstå efter"[84] ["She will give me a hint with her eyes to make me understand after"]. In her own narrative about her Scottish lover, Dundas, Iselin admits that when she looks at herself in the mirror after her encounter, she remarks "Min Gud, jeg hadde aldrig set på mig selv med de øine før"[85] ["Good God, I never looked at herself with those eyes before"]. Contributing to the aggressive way Iselin has especially in context to her amorous nature and multiple partners, Hamsun attributes Iselin with libidinal energy, as that which compels Glahn but also inspires him to act similar to her. In a similar way, Glahn mirrors Iselin's powerful form of communication with her eyes. Edvarda mentions to Glahn that her friend remarks on his intense animal eyes. Within his own psyche, Glahn also measures admiration from Edvarda, Iselin, and other women, and equates their love for him by the intensity of the eyes when they look at him. In the Norwegian text, the look is described more as a glance, putting the emphasis on the way of looking as opposed to the eyes themselves. This focus on the glance coincides with Iselin's glance to herself in the mirror when she first noticed the intensity in her eyes.

In reference to *Victoria*, Hamsun correlates Johannes's identity to Iselin in a more subtle way. During the more natural interactions between Johannes and Victoria, Hamsun writes of both characters picking flowers or walking along the forest. In addition to the aforementioned example of the start of the story, Hamsun writes about how Johannes wanders around the side of the lake, the thicket, and the quarry to pick flowers, and Victoria intentionally meets him there to invite him to the Castle party. Other instances include two narratives based on Johannes and Victoria's interactions in the thickets. In another instance, Victoria pleads to Johannes that he is the man she loves, and she indicates that she "nu holder jeg meg heller litt inne i skogen ved siden av veien; for der gikk også *han* helst"[86] ["now I rather stay a little in the woods by the side of the road; because there he [Johannes] also preferred to go there"].

In conjunction with *Pan*, Hamsun situates Johannes as belonging to the forest, a position that places Victoria as the hunter. While these examples do not directly allude to Iselin, a reader perceives the correlation of Johannes as Iselin when considering the similarities in pastoral setting that intensifies the feelings of admiration from the hunter. In this case, Johannes differs from Glahn since Glahn positions himself as a hunter who goes out to nature to contact the nature spirit, while Johannes does so to surround himself in an inspiring environment to help him with his writing. In this case, Victoria is the hunter who seeks the creative force, Johannes, in the forest. While Hamsun differs in his depiction of how his male characters mirror Iselin, the difference still infers her significance. In *Pan*, Hamsun makes his male character immerse himself in the forest to access Iselin, while in *Victoria*, he places Johannes in the forest in order to create thoughts where he can use his artistic voice, Munken Vendt to further create Iselin's love story with Diderik.

Finally, the identity of the artist arises in the form of fantasy and writing that occurs when the men start associating their creative behavior—whether through storytelling in Glahn's case or writing in Johannes's case—with their fixation on Iselin. The act of writing becomes the new ideal that the male characters relinquish their satisfaction. Lacan asserts that sublimation—in the form of art or courtly poetry—diverts libidinal energy to create a new object, superimposing the form of desire itself.[87] While Iselin remains in the background, the new vignette arises as a means to satisfy the characters. Lacanian scholar, Joan Copjec asserts that the libidinal drive seeks different objects as it has no goal, just an aim, and the object itself elicits satisfaction without direct allusion to the higher ideal.[88] Copjec explains Lacan's formulation as the drive choosing an object simply for the fact that it satisfies, as sublimation changes the nature of the object itself. When Lacan discusses the anecdote about Prevert's matchbook collection, he asserts that the act of collecting supersedes the idea of the matchbox itself. To clarify, the act of collecting becomes the satisfying act, and the matchbox an empty tool for such desire.[89]

To deal with the sudden loss of Eva, the person who shows devotion to him in the way he showed Iselin, Glahn creates an elaborate fantasy that shows the devotion in the act of desiring without necessitating the reciprocation of love. To put it briefly, the narrative shifts into first person, Glahn's personal writing, and depicts a maiden locked away into a stone tower away from a lord to whom she willingly gave. In return, the lord gave himself to another woman who cared less about his willingness to give, an aspect that intensified the lord's motivations to give more. The woman in the stone tower gives herself to the lord as the years progress in different ways, some include sewing his name, saving plaster to put in a jar as a remembrance of him, and finally thinking of him despite the fact that he does not love her. The fantasy depicts unrequited love but shows the endurance of the person suffering. The aim is to show suffering and to allude to Eva's sacrifice because she gives her devotion to Glahn despite the fact that he prefers Iselin. Hamsun shows that Glahn's identity as a writer depicts a merging of identities of the artist with his artistic ideal, Iselin. In other words, his desire for storytelling arises from the perceived traits he sees in Iselin, his artistic ideal, especially after she tells him her stories of her lovers. The collision of the two identities through the act of writing positions the libidinal impulse as the crucial signifier that distinguishes them from others. Not only does Glahn position himself as Iselin, but he also takes the role of the author depicting the original scene when Glahn first desires Iselin.

In *Victoria*, Hamsun mentions her in a line when correlating Johannes's heartbreak over Victoria's betrayal to his travels abroad. Through his poetic voice as Munken Vendt, Johannes indicates that Diderik is emphasized as someone "Gud slo med klærlighet"[90] ["God struck with love"]. Since Diderik is mentioned in relation to Iselin, a parallel to Johannes's reaction to Victoria, one can only assume that the one Diderik loves is Iselin. Near the end of the novel before Johannes tells Camilla to go with Richmond, he describes to her his fairytale end as consisting with an hour of love. Titling it, "Slekten" ["The Genus" or "The Spirit of Life"], Johannes exuberantly tells Camilla that every creature in the forest has an hour of love. He mentions that this fantasy is finally written down, as he has experienced the vision once more. He states, "En bølge av henrykkelse er ivente, øynene blir ildfullere, barmene ånder. Så stiger en fin rødme opp fra jorden; det er unnselighetens rødme fra alle de nakne hjerter, og natten farves rosenrød."[91] ["A wave of rapture awaits, their eyes become more fiery, bosoms breathe. Then a fine blush rises up from the earth, it is the blush of kindness from all those naked hearts, and the night has a rosy red color."]

Johannes' obsession with writing diminishes his sense of reality, as he depicts scenes from "Slekten/The Genus/The Spirit of Life." In the Norwegian text, the title refers to "The Genus," meaning the second to the last name in the biological classification system. Typically the genus is the common name for a living creature, a group prior to any living creature's specific species. By writing Johannes' story as "The Genus," Hamsun intends to unify all the living creatures. Considering that Johannes discusses the hour of creation when all appears red, the term *genus* refers to part of the identity of living beings, as living beings are named with the genus, then the species. The focus is on the method of creation, similar to the hour of love mentioned in Glahn's hour with Iselin in *Pan*. Not only has he written his identity and desire into the story, but also Johannes depicts how the goal of desire is to maintain the feeling of attraction, as seen in the form of a representation of love deeply felt between two characters but held apart by stubbornness. The imagery here parallels the first scene with Iselin in *Pan*, where the sun arises from the sea in that one hour. The delicate blush and rose-red hue mirrors the color of the sky when Glahn has his hour with Iselin. In both *Pan* and *Victoria*, Iselin functions as a synecdoche for all forest creatures, her eyes growing more rapturous and ardent. It seems to refer to the rapture that Glahn experiences in the forest when the forest comes alive. Johannes, unlike Glahn, uses his fantasies to successfully turn his feelings of loss into stories.

After Victoria's fiancé dies, Johannes writes smaller fairytale stories, the one in particular is about the mother in blue with two dark-haired daughters who love the same man. Depicting a love triangle in which the older sister loves the man who in return loves the younger sister, Johannes inserts himself as the man who pleads to the younger sister, who reluctantly refuses him. While one might debate that Johannes writes the younger sister as Victoria, the small vignette occurs prior to Camilla's visit to Johannes when she tells him that she spent the entire time dancing with Richmond. When taking into consideration that Victoria sets up Johannes with Camilla just as the older sister advised the man to speak to the younger sister, one perceives that Johannes inserts Camilla's character as the younger sister in his story. Regardless of the character depiction, Johannes becomes wholly engrossed in his writing, foregoing a reaction against Camilla's evident feelings for Richmond. For Johannes, the idea of life and spring, the libidinal investment in Iselin, shows an elaboration of the devotion bestowed upon Victoria through Johannes' writing. Depicting love as originally coming to earth on a spring night when a young man sees two eyes and kisses two lips and describing it as "en sol som lynte mot en stjerne"[92] ["a sun that casts lightning bolts at a star"], Johannes describes a love that arises from the beginning of time, thus harkening back to the Iselin of four generations ago.

As seen in Boasson's description of vitalism as an impulsive bond to nature, Hamsun writes about Glahn as becoming part of nature and trying to find life after social conventions destroy nature. According to Boasson, the close association between literature and nature suggests Hamsun's vitalistic goal of allowing nature to speak to one's senses. Hamsun uses the character, Iselin, as a way to show the natural impulses or the unconscious factors that humans are only sensitive to if they are akin to nature.[93] Through the midnight sun experience, nature grows with the extra sun exposure. Benjamin Bigelow explains that the focus on the sun worship arises in the idea that the sun's rays promote good health and vitality for the soul. According to Bigelow, Hamsun adheres to a vitalism that is more focused on the combination of the psychological and physiological experience of the body. By providing context of the realism and scientific empiricism of the latter half of the nineteenth century, he shows how Hamsun takes on the vitalism, or vital materialism, whose manifestations on the human body reveal its departure from pure Romanticism.[94] Hamsun may be enacting the paradoxical quality of desire as that which attracts and repulses him when he writes of the simultaneous way that Johannes saves Victoria in his writing, despite his inability to save her at the end. Johannes focuses more on the symbolic nature that Iselin, as a symbol of life, might incur on his art. He does this by infusing his own fantasies and writing with references to light and life. In this way, Johannes differs from Glahn in so far as his object of desire is Victoria, and Iselin only functions as a creative expression. Johannes uses his poetic voice as Munken Vendt to describe Iselin as a nature creature and an object of desire for Diderik. Iselin becomes more of a creation within a story that parallels Johannes's bond with Victoria.

Though I do not describe Iselin from *Munken Vendt*, the drama, in detail, it is worth mentioning that she tortures her beloved, Munken Vendt, in a natural setting, the woods. Instead of showing her more tender aspects, Iselin in *Munken Vendt* is beautiful yet cold and proudly tortures Munken Vendt despite her feelings of affection for him. Buttry suggests Munken's initial refusal of Iselin as motivation for Iselin's decision to torture him by binding him to a tree and binding his hands filled with dirt and seed for several days.[95] She disagrees with Arntzen's assessment of Iselin in *Munken Vendt*, as a "mother figure, symbol of fertility and destruction."[96] Through Iselin's torture of Munken Vendt, she forces him to be part of nature, thus subverting her sensuous role in the previous novels. If Arntzen is correct in his assessment of Iselin, her depiction as a destructive force fulfills the cycle of Iselin as a symbol of creation and destruction in relation to nature. Furthermore, as a cold and powerful woman, Iselin of *Munken Vendt*, enacts her destructive role, one that involves the backdrop of nature.

Pan and *Victoria* both address the way that sensuous nature prevails over the social norms mandated in social interactions. Iselin functions as the sensuous and natural form that inspires the men, Johannes and Glahn, to depict her in writing and storytelling. This devotion to writing correlates to the writing fetishism that von Schnurbein discusses. In her explanation of writing fetishism, she shows how Glahn as a lonely wanderer finds two mythological nature spirits, Iselin and Diderik, who function as fetishized objects of nature. Since the fantasies are told from Glahn's perspective, it also portrays the fetish of a storyteller.[97] Von Schnurbein describes the example of the blind woman in the tower who foolishly awaits her lover as a symbol for Glahn's own guilt over his taking part of Eva's death. Moreover, the woman in the tower who pines for her absent lover also symbolizes Glahn's feelings of loss In regard to Edvarda,[98] Hamsun uses a similar technique in *Victoria*. His minor stories function as symbols of Johannes's sad feelings about losing Victoria and to a certain extent, Camilla.

Furthermore, the stories become emblematic of the aesthetic process in artistic creation. Indeed, von Schnurbein comments that the mini narratives within the novels show how "all artistic creativity, all narration remains dependent on the same 'perverse' fetishistic and thus both modern and 'primitive' structure that the texts criticize."[99] In other words, she criticizes the contradiction in the layering of narratives and its function as serving as a critical way to comment on the main narrative. Yet, in her valid assessment of Hamsun's early work, she diminishes the relevance of the writing fetish. By minimizing them as only fetishes, she lessens the importance in the view of Iselin as a creative force and symbol of fertility. It diminishes the view of Iselin as a compelling life force and relegates her to mere male fantasy. Moreover, Glahn's and Johannes' stories express desire but are also products of this desire. While she makes a valid assessment of Hamsun's early work, the reader interprets her notion of the fetish gaze as the internal struggle within an artist in which Hamsun depicts to clarify the psychological process within a creative person. Even if he does portray food fetish, sexual fetish, and writing as fetish through his work, Hamsun's use of them portrays the different signifiers in the artistic process. He shows how the artist takes aspects from nature and reattributes newer meaning through the creative act of writing. Iselin becomes a fetish in his story but also a metonym for nature and the way that both Glahn and Johannes find inspiration in Iselin, for she embodies nature.

Jan Sjåvik further incorporates a Freudian analysis of a writer's fantasy when he states that the author satisfies his desire to write his narrative in a particular way to control the reader's interpretation of it.[100] He refers to another point he made about how a main theme in *Pan* was the connection between writing and sexual activity. Alexandra Columban mentions that the unconsummated love between Glahn and Edvarda inspires the creative activity, which implies that the sublimated drive shifts into writing.[101] While her point is to discuss the myth of the artist in Hamsun's work, it also supports the idea that Hamsun intended to comment on the role of artistic creation. If Hamsun is discussing the control of having his readers interpret his work a certain way, he is exploring the way that writers use libidinal energy to push the writer toward a goal even if its process leads to unexpected confrontation with different symbols. In her article, "The Muse and the Mimosa: Knut Hamsun's Portrayal of the Inspired Artist," Buttry describes how Hamsun incorporates aspects of divine inspiration but clarifies that the sensitivity required from accessing the divine is the inner self that finds the creative inspiration. She expresses the relevance of the mystical and mythological presence as the creative inspiration that Hamsun's characters find certain aspects within themselves.[102] Collectively, many views of Hamsun's early work address a turn to nature away from social concerns, a process that eventually transforms art, a human-made product, into one of nature.

A Lacanian view of *Pan* and *Victoria* shows the relevance of vitalism, especially in the connection among nature, love, and art that aforementioned scholars discuss in their work. Considering that Hamsun rewrote the myth of Pan through his creation of Iselin, the relevance of Lacanian sublimation becomes more pertinent, especially when considering Lacan's comment on the myth:

> Pan pursues the nymph Syrinx, who runs away from him and disappears among the reeds. In his rage, he cuts down the reeds, and that, Longus tells us, is the origin of the flute with pipes of unequal length—Pan wanted, the subtle poet adds, to express in that way the fact that his love was without equal. Syrinx is transformed into the pipe of pan's flute.[103]

Lacan expresses how Pan changes the form of the Syrinx into an object that channels artistic energy into sound. In conducting a Lacanian analysis of Iselin's energy onto the male writer, one discovers a similar structure that Lacan describes in his use of Pan as the model for sublimation. Inherent in transformation is the destruction of a creative force into another object, the flute that inspires more creativity. This exploration of nature as embodied within a female ideal, Iselin, shows that admiration of her also includes admiration of nature. When the male characters engage with nature and Iselin, their creative thinking about them channels their particular experiences with the forest. Hamsun's vitalistic goal emerges through the act of writing, as a way one could express intimacy through one's inspiration from nature. I pose the question whether sublimation, as I recently depicted here as a distinction from its traditional meaning, transforms desire for nature in such a way that artists simultaneously depict and enact it.

Illustration: Sea Holly with Light

Chapter 3

Death's Symbol: The Lyktemann's Daughter

In *Mysterier*, Hamsun introduces his eccentric protagonist, Johan Nagel, who develops stories to simultaneously lure the women in a small town and mystify his own sense of self. Unlike Glahn in *Pan*, Nagel partakes in social gatherings where he delivers the long monologues that reveal strange personal stories and political views, none meant to be taken seriously. Throughout the long novel, Nagel falls in love with two women in the story, young Dagny and older Martha, who are simultaneously fascinated yet frustrated with him. Nagel's stories mystify the reader's perception of his character, and his telling of the fairytale to Dagny, his first crush, is the most compelling of the novel. Nagel creates a myth for Dagny, and then, a mythical identity for himself. Insofar as his feelings for her and later for Martha, are sublimated into beautiful poetic phrases filled details of life and death symbolism, a reader can take note that such sublimation takes a deeper degree in this story due to the fact that Nagel does not consummate his sexual inclinations with anyone.

To clarify on sublimation, its depictions in *Mysterier* differentiate from the Lacanian influence as discussed in the chapter on Iselin. As a preface, Nagel's association with nature, erotic feelings for Dagny, and storytelling tendencies compares to Glahn's feelings in the forest, erotic feelings for different women, and storytelling techniques. Nagel's sublimation functions more as a result of blind faith in his own ego-ideal, a version of himself that he postulates to the women of a party. Nagel does transform his erotic feelings for Dagny into a story, and as a result, he captures her attention, but shortly after, he resorts to his impulsive self again. In Nagel's case, unlike Glahn and Johannes, his sublimation of his feelings and creation of a fanciful story indicates Nagel's ideal self—his ego-ideal—yet the constant battle between his idealized self and his darker repressed passions cause him to succumb to darker impulses and the end of his life.

For the purpose of this discussion, Freud's initial distinction between ego formation and sublimation helps clarify one's understanding of Nagel's use of the fairytale, a detail not generally discussed In his early essay "On Narcissism," Freud mentions, "It is true that the ego ideal demands such sublimation, but it cannot enforce it; sublimation remains a special process which can be prompted by the ideal but the execution of which is entirely independent of such prompting."[104] In other words, sublimation does influence a person's behavior to achieve noble feats, yet the person's goal changes from satisfying a sexual instinct. Freud further clarifies that sublimation offers a person a way out of repression. In Nagel's case, it is precisely his inability to maintain this ideal that makes him fall victim to more repression.

In his book, *Sublimation,* Hans W. Loewald's assessment of sublimation as a reconciliation between the ego and the passions explains for Nagel's use of the fairytale. While Freud might indicate that sublimation is apart from the execution process of creative discovery, Loewald suggests that the ego formation itself constitutes the sublimation process. Loewald asserts "an essential ingredient in sublimation is the higher value of certain aims and objects, including the value of the ego itself as a higher form of psychic organization and human development."[105] Nagel's attempt to use his fairytale as a formation of a better version of himself explains how he uses words to capture Dagny's attention. For the moment that he does captivate her, Nagel believes his storytelling ambitions provides him, thus showing credibility in the formation of his ego. Unlike my discussion of Glahn's sublimation, Nagel presents a fairytale that functions as a mythology of himself. Thus, he goes a step further than Glahn who merely takes on some of Iselin's actions. Within one small part of the novel, Nagel demonstrates his inner struggle with life and death, and his appeal to Dagny through the fairytale epitomizes the idealized beauty and his true potential.

Part of Nagel's process of creating a myth is his ability to state the

Norwegian huldre as a pedestrian version of folktales in contrast to the Chinese dragon before taking on some of the huldre's abilities. Nagel mentions that the Norwegian folktales are commonplace and set in the countryside as opposed to some magical place. His behavior, however, shows how he presents himself as a mythological creature, as he uses his tale to cunningly lure the women, especially Dagny.

According to Reidar Christiansen's *Folktales of Norway*, the huldre is a supernatural maiden who belongs to the huldre-folk, or the hidden people. They live at the borders of the forest and human shelter, either at the edge of a small village or city. The term "huldre" derives from hylja, which denotes "to cover" or to "conceal."[106] Various Norwegian folktales depict huldres as a being that strikes some caution, marking a distinction between huldre people and humans. Some folktales reveal huldres to love mortals, but such romantic hopes often leave the mortal with misfortune and insanity. Some involve less menacing huldres who help humans with their changeling infants and animal herding. Two of the ones involving men marrying huldres reflect an inability to think reasonably or go about their lives. In addition to having an irresistible power in courtship, the huldres also possess different magical powers, such as the abilities to disappear and reappear, to heal others, and to transform other beings. Some have the gift of foresight. Many items associated with huldres depict a similar notion of magical aspects. Regardless of such scant details, the huldre possesses spectacular powers even though she affects those people in seemingly ordinary settings.

In this example, Nagel indirectly compares himself to the female huldre whose foxtail she hides from the human male mate. Instead of hiding a tail as a huldre would, Nagel uses his tales as a way to hide his affection but also present his identity as a myth. He conceals his affection and identity while presenting a different meaning to Dagny in order to lure her. Coinciding with the huldre's affinity for nature, he cites how much he belongs to the forest. When saying how happy he is in Dagny's company, he says, "Det er som om jeg var en del av denne skog eller denne mark, en gren på en furu eller en sten, gjærne en sten også, men en sten som var gjennemtrængt av al denne fine duft og fred som omgir os..."[107] [It is as if I were part of this forest or this field, a branch on a pine tree or a stone, yes, preferably a stone too, but a stone that was permeated with all this fine fragrance and peace that surround us…]. Each time he sees Dagny or feels a profound feeling of sexual awakening, Nagel refers to the forest, not a far cry from Glahn's love of the forest.

Prior to his attendance to the social gathering where he will later tell the fairytale, Nagel experiences a powerful emotion in response to nature. On the Midsummer Eve when the midnight sun is out the longest time of the year, Nagel experiences a wonderful feeling, one that connects to his love for nature and light. Concerning Nagel's state of mind, Hamsun writes:

> Han var i en gåtefuld tilstand, fyldt av psykisk behag; hver nerve i ham var våken, han fornam musik i sit blod, følte sig beslægtet med hele natur, med solen og fjældene og alt andet, kjendte sig omsuset av sin egen jegfølelse fra trær og tuvet og strå. Hans sjæl blev stor og fuldtonenede som et orgel inde i ham of aldrig glemte han hvorledes den milde musik likefrem gled op og ned i hans blod.[108]
>
> [He was in an enigmatic state, filled with psychic pleasure; every nerve in him was awake, he felt music in his blood, felt related to all nature, to the sun and the mountains and everything else, felt surrounded by his own sense of self from trees and tufts and straw. His soul became large and full-toned like an organ inside him, and he never forgot how the gentle music just glided up and down in his blood.]

In this scene, he demonstrates signs of inspiration from nature, as he feels every nerve in him awakened through the sensation of seeing the trees, tufts and leaves. As his soul gets bigger within him, he cannot explain this passionate energy he feels. Since he terms it as "enigmatic," he considers his kinship as mysterious and unusual to most of the people in the small town. The psychic pleasure refers to the wild passion of nature that stirs within him, similar to Glahn's feeling in the forest. This sensation marks the happiest time that Nagel experiences in the novel, as he is alone to reflect on the different forms of nature that inspire him. The specific impact on Nagel's identity, "focus on sense of self" or "kjendte sig omsuset av sin egen jegfølelse," clearly demonstrates his true sense of being while surrounded by trees, mountains, the sun, and other venery. In the Norwegian version, the translation is "feels the rage of his own self-esteem," which denotes a more dramatic effect of nature on him. The rage indicates how akin the scenery is to him, a fact that Nagel attempts to allude to in his own abilities to create beautiful imagery with words. This focus on the self alludes to Atle Kittang's interpretation of the narcissistic fantasy with nature. Not only is the fantasy about his own connection to nature, but also the experience itself contributes to Nagel's sense of self. An optimistic interpretation could be that this sensuous experience portrays Nagel's true comfort with himself, that he is one with the forest as opposed to feeling this way with other people, despite his inclinations toward Dagny.

Referring to the psychological aspect of Nagel's experience with nature, Kittang asserts that the text refers to some return of a projected view of himself onto nature, thus alluding to the narcissistic aspect to this fantasy. Kittang furthers this connection between them when describing how the interaction itself demonstrates a contraction and expansion between Nagel and the natural world.[109] Kittang portrays that Nagel does engage in the same type of behavior as the fantasy entails mainly an experience of nature on Nagel's sense of self. Furthermore, when Nagel mentions that he feels "musik i sitt blod" [music in his blood], he asserts that the sensation of music refers to the dissolution of the ego in the imagination, the boundary where lies his sense of self.[110] Although Kittang refers to this phenomenon as traces of death and destruction, I refer to it as his fascination of himself as existing outside the perimeters of a human experience. Thus, in his inability to sense music in his blood—though Hamsun does prescribe a metaphorical meaning—Nagel professes to feel a sensation beyond human capabilities. In a sense, though he might feel as if he has music in his blood, Nagel does not actually feel it. In this allusion to a death of Nagel's human abilities, Hamsun also expresses Nagel's yearning to believe in a lie. In his connection with nature, Nagel experiences a fantasy of an identity, or an ontology that merges with nature, thus concealing his death of his human self from his own awareness. It is his unconscious wills that hide his desire of death from his conscious awareness. In his conscious awareness, he only recognizes his will to mythicize his identity through his words, hence showing similar trends in his words to Dagny as he did in his fantasy.

In the party scene prior to telling his fairytale, Nagel demonstrates his ability to play with symbols and creates a beautiful scene. By portraying beautiful scenery, he begins his journey to presenting himself as a confident and poetic man, one whose sensibilities provides Dagny with a memorable detail that she uses to defend against all other inconsistences in his character. Describing a dream, Nagel charms Dagny as well as the other women in the party by stating "båt av duftende træ of med et seil av lyseblå silke, klippet i halvmåne"[111] [a boat of flagrant wood with a sail of pale-blue silk cut in the shape of a crescent moon]. Despite the poetic quality of his words, however, Kittang asserts that they refer to death, as it is a small section that is part of a larger story that details how the subject is on a boat already rocking on the sea to heaven. He further addresses that Nagel's poetic words to Dagny, in combination with Nagel's previous erotic fantasy with light, depict a sign of decomposition and frustration despite its paradoxical beauty and erotic fantasy.[112]

In fact, in *Hele Livet en Vandrer i Naturen,* Henning Howlid Wærp conducts a close reading of Nagel's meetings with Dagny and Martha in order to ascertain the Nagel's reliability. Investigating deeply into the chronology of events, Wærp aptly proves the inconsistences of the plot in *Mysterier* since Nagel imagines his meetings with Dagny and Martha. Showing that the novel reveals a mixture of imagined events and reality and poem and prose, Wærp concludes that Nagel creates his perception based on illusions as part of his creative faculties.[113] Taking this direction, I consider the dreamlike fairytale, an example of Nagel's creative inventions and consider its deeper implications in a psychoanalytic dimension. By exploring the symbolic meaning of Nagel's fairytale and allusion to mythology, a reader perceives Nagel's feelings as a social outcast and as someone who belongs with nature. Expanding on Wærp's observation of Nagel's world as transgressing the borders of reality and dreams, I hint how his allusions indicate a loss of belief in himself by a full immersion into fantasy.

Split in Identity

While demonstrating a different interpretation than a pure Lacanian sublimation, Nagel's fairytale reveals a split between the personae that he wishes to project and his real identity. In *The Four Fundamental Ideas in Psychoanalysis*, Lacan explains his notion of the split in identity, which he explicates as the difference between being and meaning or the difference between enunciated (the speaker) and the enunciation (the statement). The first occurs because the subject is born into language that is dependent on particular meanings apart from the speaker's conscious intentions. The speaker of the enunciation differs from the enunciation itself.

Without bringing too many examples of the negation where Lacan explains this difference, his view can be summarized as the difference between the enunciated and the enunciation is similar to the disappearance of the subject in desire. A person who desires makes a comment, and the comment takes hold over the person. The meaning that arises through the use of symbols from each male character functions as the significant issues arising when the male characters as subjects disappear and enter into a kind of death as subjects who lose agency through signifiers.[114] In other words, a speaker's words themselves become the focal point of one's conversation, as opposed to the person who utters them. One examines this difference between Nagel's fairytale and his own agency, and through this exploration, one perceives unforeseen powers he bestows to women as life-giving beings.

This particular difference—his desire for myth and his confrontation with his real self—could be furthered explained as the difference between meaning and being in speech. While in being, he opens up about his strange actions and mysterious intentions, as traits that define him, yet he also feels the beauty of the forest and in Dagny's presence that inspires him to produce his meaning, a man of myth. The fairytale further shows the interpretation of Nagel as a mythological creature that furthers the discussion of him as a huldre. His tales in the setting of the forest as the backdrop put him in the role of a mythological creature, as someone who rejects human categorization. It is the identity he wishes to have, as opposed to the human one that scars him. While Nagel is communicating his desires through the content of his dream, his delivery shows his mythological nature and his goal to present himself as myth.

Through Nagel's fairytale of the Lyktemann's daughter, Hamsun reveals Nagel's desire for both the betrothed mortal woman, Dagny, and his love for the forest. As in the previous legend of the imprisoned woman in *Pan*, the devotion that Nagel instills both in the fairytale and in his devotion to Dagny incurs loss. Although the fairytale reveals the height of Nagel's motivation to create a mythological story, the story itself shows the power of the female mythological that Nagel internalizes and through the blind fairy. Kittang further asserts how Nagel's fairytale demonstrates the tension between Nagel's identity and his sense of alienation and a combination of themes of love and death.[115] On the one hand, it portrays the sensuous landscape and beautiful music against a backdrop of a dark octagonal tower and a menacing Lyktemann who does not want his daughter to welcome Nagel. As I will explain further, the daughter, the blind fairy, is the object of love for Nagel, but her expression of her love for him entails her death.

Regarding Nagel's ability to craft a beautiful story, Buttry's asserts how Hamsun's characters portray their deep sensitivities that enable them to access an internalized subconscious creative impulse. In her article, "The Muse and the Mimosa," Buttry examines Hamsun's stories and his personal letters and looks at the role of nature, art, and his sensitivity functions as a conduit to artistic expression.[116] Buttry analyzes the trend in Hamsun's writing that details failed erotic pursuits as the means that puts the characters into such emotional states similar to a drugged state. The feeling of love and euphoria is a preliminary step to find the artistic inspiration, as if a sign from the divine is to test the artist prior to giving the inspiration. With this view, a reader perceives how Nagel's fairy-tale develops from his inspiration from nature but also from his need to impress Dagny. In this particular instance, he uses the conflict of Dagny's unavailability to propel him to talk to her of beautiful imagery, thus showing how friction in this conflict puts him in a euphoric state that inspires an artful tale.

As a mirrored statement to his previous observation, Ingar Sletten Kolloen writes about Hamsun's male characters: "Nagel, Glahn, and the central figure in *Hunger* had all failed to capture the women they loved. And any of his characters who had been affianced or married had always suffered betrayal."[117] Kolloen is apt to make such an assessment of Hamsun's work, as it proved to be a reflection of the Hamsun's thoughts on the modern women and his own preoccupation with how disinterested he becomes once he captures his women. Regarding the novels *Hunger*, *Mysteries* and *Pan*, Kolloen notes "love would be kept potent through fantasy and poetry and, in turn, that ideal of love would fuel words and art."[118]

Thus, Nagel's feelings in regard to Dagny fuel his fantasy as being part of nature and expressing this as a key reason why he was given entry into the scene where the fairytale takes places. Regardless of whether Nagel is sincere in his words, his fairytale paradoxically reveals yet also conceals Nagel's wishes. He uses the story as a figurative device to shield the terror of love but also proclaim it at the same time.

The Fairytale of Lantern Man's Daughter

In particular, Nagel's fairytale hints at his wish to present a myth of himself as opposed to presenting his true wish to consider suicide, yet he hides this facet from the group of women. Early on in the novel, Nagel tells a small party of women a story, yet het directs it to Dagny. He describes one winter's night when he was interrupted from reading by a voice that beckoned him. He perceived a small man with a red beard and luminous light also concealed himself, so Nagel followed him as the small man leads Nagel through the forest. As they get deeper into the forest, the little man pushed Nagel forward, leading him to a black octagonal tower. A crucial detail is the look of terror in the little man's eyes, as he paradoxically leads yet pushes away Nagel. A young woman with red hair and dark eyes approached them, and she took light from the tiny man, whom Nagel describes as part human, part animal. The detail about how she takes light is significant: she searches throughout the little man's clothing and finds a flame of light. She brings the light to Nagel, showing how it hangs from her fingers. Then she tells Nagel to take off his shoes and clothes in order to dry from the dew outside. Despite the fact that she lies to her father, she does so to protect Nagel. Showing her chaste nature, she asks him to take off his clothes but does not engage in sexual activity with him.

So far, details about this fairytale coincides with other legends of the Lyktemann. Later, once Nagel goes away from the tower after that night, he does find out from his maid that the identity of this man is indeed the Lyktemann, the bad soul rejected from Hell who lives in the tower with his daughter. In the Norwegian text, Hamsun writes of this man as "Lyktemann," the legend of the man who uses lights to lure mortals into the marsh. If the mortals fall to their death, the legend gains power in cautioning others not to wander into the marsh at night. In some European legends, the lights from the Lantern Man refer to spirits who cannot enter into the afterlife, thus they are meant to wander in the form of light. One might infer that the daughter has an evil motive, despite showing him otherwise through her kind actions and her protection over Nagel during his night there. Given that both the woman and the Lyktemann have light in the form of a flame, a detail that matches the different legends of this bad spirit, a reader infers the likelihood that both creatures lack access to the afterlife.

During the second part of the fairytale, Nagel shifts the mood of the tale from suspenseful and terrifying to wonder and amazement. He hears beautiful music during the night as little fairies fly around in the tower. At that moment, the fairytale takes some significance to the beauty in music and light. Similar to Glahn's sexual adventure with Iselin at 1 a.m. in the morning, Nagel notes that the lovely music and sight of tiny naked fairies fluttering around in darkness occurs at 1 a.m. Using a focus on the supernatural, Nagel describes it as "en sælsom, overnaturlig nydelse"[119] [a rare mysterious supernatural pleasure]. The appearance of the fairies fills him with happiness, a feeling that eventually lulls him into sleep. In the morning, Nagel mentions that the fairy told him that she sang during the night when the fairies flew around him. This contrast between the initial scary sight of the Lyktemann and the beauty of the light from the fairies gives this fairytale its protagonist and antagonist. The Lyktemann, the antagonist, lures Nagel from his home with a seemingly nefarious reason, yet the blind fairy saves him from the Lyktemann's grasp.

The next day, the fairy furthers her protection over Nagel. As he leaves, he gives the woman two kisses on her forehead, and she gives him her black ribbon that he ties around the wrist. She cries and asks him if he sees his town, and then he declares his love for her. After describing her as beautiful with the sunlight on her hair and "hendes sorte øine var herlige"[120] [her black eyes were lovely], he falls at her feet after kissing her. This act induces her to give him her black ribbon and a sad feeling, inducing tears. Her power makes him proclaim, "Hvor du gjør mig glad i dig, hvor du fyller mig med lykke!"[121] [How you make me happy within you, how you fill me with happiness!]. Nagel never qualifies his love for her, but only states it after she cries.

Despite a loss of the ability to see in the mortal sense, she offers him the sight of magical fairies flying around him, the revelation of different souls. This power that separates him from the mythological world helps her situate when Nagel is closer to his city, so when she asks him if he could see the outskirts of the town, she knows that their bond is nearly over. This power of spatial distance as equating an end to their short-term relationship conveys knowledge that the supernatural female knows that Nagel does not. Thus, the power of her eyes, like Iselin's, symbolizes life, though the fairy uses her sight for Nagel's sake, not her own. Nagel confesses that he leaves the site, only to return to find the blind fairy.

A few days after, however, Nagel returns to the site and encounters the unexpected. He finds the woman dead while Lyktemann lives. Nagel perceives her dead body and her father watching over it. Despite the little information on her, one knows that she gave Nagel entry into her room and offered him a supernatural experience, and then, led him back to his town, as he had wandered too far. If one takes into account the myth of the Lantern spirits, she was a spirit who could not travel to the afterlife until her father killed her. By giving her the power of life in the form of her sacrifice, Hamsun imbues the character as a form of life, libidinal energy, thus showing that the power of the female is to give life. Her foresight and ability to perceive spatial distance reflects the way that her blindness allows her to see paths that mortals cannot. Though this depiction of the coveted woman demonstrates traditionally feminine aspects, as seen in her beauty and sacrifice of her life, her role as life giving supersedes Nagel's role in the creation of his myth.

While the story itself signifies Nagel's affection for Dagny, the blind fairy's qualities themselves transcend the tale, as she creates the beauty of the dark octagonal tower. Her vision to help Nagel counter the darker forces of that tower saves him but more importantly allows him to enter into the liminal space. Nagel is within his town yet also in a structure that has supernatural aspects. This supernatural woman either a blind fairy or the daughter of a demon gives him the power to partake of the liminal space yet also leave it when necessary. I have analyzed her role in the story and her symbolic meaning as a part of Nagel's story to Dagny and the other women at the party. Thus, many readers perceive how the blind fairy's inability to be with Nagel exposes Hamsun's trend of writing ill-fated relationships.

The Fairytale as a Sign of the Struggle in Self-Belief

Nagel sublimates his desire for Dagny by crafting a beautiful fairytale, and an analysis of the key characters helps to show how the death of Lykteman's daughter foreshadows Nagel's lack of belief in his ego ideal, or the subject's form of ego that is built upon the subject's social interactions with others and incorporation of society's roles into the subject's mind.[122] To be more specific, the ego ideal is one form of the ego that is based on the symbolic connection one develops through social interactions, or the way that we define ourselves through the use of words in speech with another person.

In terms of Nagel's use of the story to symbolize his feelings for Dagny, a reader interprets his story as a creation of a myth and a means to charm Dagny and the other women at the party. By describing the blind woman with reddish golden hair, he attributes her beauty and kindness to Dagny, as both are both women he cannot have. Both female characters attempt to perceive the best in him; the blind fairy tries to save him by tying a black ribbon around his wrist, while Dagny consistently asks for reasons why he reveals his trickery. Her constant inquiry, though motivated by her curiosity of Nagel's intentions for his lies, functions as subtle hints to save him from confessing his lies to her. By wishing to believe that part of Nagel's beauty in his words and deeper implications of his use of symbols, Dagny embodies the reader's desire to combine Nagel's identity with his ability to create meaning through symbols. Furthermore, Lyktemann's daughter is blind, and her blindness alludes to Dagny's blind sense of perception when she sees potential in the correlation between the beauty in Nagel's words and attributes them to his personality. It shows the blindness she initially has when she wants to believe in the validity of the stories but also the truth that they might reveal secrets about Nagel's identity.

The black ribbon symbolizes the protection Lyktemann's daughter holds over him, as Nagel has visited the supernatural world and cannot be part of it. Yet, the ribbon also has an inverse meaning. It symbolizes Nagel's beautiful stories that offer Dagny temporary entry into a mythological world, though she, like Nagel in his story, belongs to the human world. In this interpretation, Nagel mixes up the symbols, as he assumes the fairy's position, especially in the sense that his stories provide beautiful imagery to Dagny tantamount to the way the fairy's singing elicited feelings from Nagel. For this reason, despite Dagny's engagement and her persistent questioning for clarity of his intentions, she still wishes to understand his meaning and being as one coherent entity, only she finds a contradiction. Every time Dagny tries to makes sense of Nagel, he fumbles with different statements that contradict Nagel's intentions if he wishes to paint a favorable impression on her. This fairytale, however, takes the beauty of the forest and equates it to Dagny's beauty, instead of functioning as a way to get to Dagny. Nagel shifts between his willingness to believe in his own myth and the confrontation of his feelings of his real situation, a lonely stranger.

As much as Dagny mirrors Lyktemann's daughter, the fairy also symbolizes Nagel's good intentions, his creation, or his higher self. The fairytale depicts a struggle within himself to believe in the more aspirational self, his myth of himself. Through beautiful imagery, he composes a dream much like Nagel describes the sound of music coming from the fairies during his night at the octagonal tower.

Alluding to his bond with nature, Nagel does show some harmonic connection between death and happiness,[123] as his experience with nature shows a loss of the notion of Nagel's selfhood, or his experience as a human. While Kittang presents Nagel's preoccupation with death, I consider his analysis to further assert how his use of language pushes him to adopt a persona while disregarding his true preoccupation with death. His lovely words show how Nagel has an otherworldly demeanor, at least he wishes to give this impression to Dagny to avoid his own problems. For example, Nagel carries with him a small flask of hydrochloric acid in his coat pocket throughout his early interactions with the townspeople. Given that this proclivity alludes to a suicidal wish, Nagel diverts his attention from his death wish and offers the women, especially Dagny, beautiful imagery. After he gains the attention of an active audience, Nagel begins to construct his identity as a myth by alluding to the different folkloric traditions from other countries and telling a beautiful story that comments on the entire novel. Kittang's assessment refers his split between the meaning of his words and his identity, as the act of putting meaning into words as Nagel does entails a cut into his subjectivity—his state of being. On a linguistic level, he disappears into the meaning of his words, thus alluding to death of his identity He loses his agency as a person, as the women only pay attention to the imagery he presents as opposed to his personality.

So far, a reader achieves the interpretation of the fairytale as Nagel's creation of myth to cover his true identity as a psychologically fragile person. When perceiving this tale as another example of sublimation of Nagel's desire, readers perceive this story as Nagel's defeat in capturing Dagny, as she is already engaged to a man of an admirable status. Both of these interpretations make use of how Hamsun portrays the shift in energy and motivation to deal with his inner conflict. For Kittang, Nagel's struggle with love shows his inner conflict to feel akin to nature yet also wish to partake in social interaction due to the implications that love entails participation of two parties.[124] Kittang asserts that the octagonal structure symbolizes the father figure that presents the conflict for Nagel to fight for his Lyktemann's daughter,[125] even though Nagel presents her as someone who sacrifices herself for Nagel's survival. Thus, Nagel does not show his ability to fight as a hero, yet his abilities to deflect to her in order to save him. While Nagel is successful in presenting an erotic and sensuous tale that moves women, he also demonstrates how he constantly wavers between death and destruction on one side and love and life on the other. He shows that he cannot save himself. For Nagel, the libidinal drive is more focused on ego and building of an ego as opposed to his pursuit for Dagny and then later in the novel his pursuit of Martha.

As a final note, a reader cannot ignore the presence of Lyktemann himself, a figure who symbolizes Minutten, the dwarf social outcast in the northern Norwegian town Nagel visits. At first, Nagel tries to help and defend him from the police and other townspeople, yet he quickly finds that his dreams about Minutten trouble him and show Minutten's hidden nature. Minutten is Nagel's ego-ideal, his uncanny double, despite that uncanny doubles usually entails two characters who look almost identical. While Nagel and Minutten look very different, they resemble each other in their mysterious personalities, thus making Minutten Nagel's uncanny double on a symbolic level. From Nagel's first encounter with Minutten, he shows mercy on him and tries to uncover why the others mistreat him. Throughout the novel, Nagel creates his identity as myth, despite Minutten's watchful eye over him. Nagel's fate, his death, occurs due to his confrontation with his symbolic double. As an aside, Hamsun includes a dwarf character in his novel, *Victoria*. In the beginning of the novel, the main character, Johannes has a fantasy of a being a king of his realm and has a dwarf as his servant who kneels before him. Young Johannes has this fantasy to alleviate his feelings of rejection after the titular character, Victoria, rejects his offer to carry her off the boat. Since Johannes' ego was wounded, he needed to create the image of the dwarf to show that someone is subservient to him. After this scene, however, the dwarf does not appear since Johannes matures into a thoughtful and sensitive writer. Similar to young Johannes, Nagel requires the company of the dwarf as a means of a contrast to his own personality. Upon closer examination, however, a reader perceives that Minutten symbolizes a part of Nagel's identity that he does not want to recognize in himself.

Regarding the discussion of the uncanny double, Mladen Dolar explains how the double functions as that figure who has the "object a" of the subject, as opposed to functioning as the object of desire. Moreover, Dolar states that the double functions as that which disrupts the subject's path to pleasure and his desire. As Mladen Dolar explains, the subject is separated from his self-recognition and his jouissance, or enjoyment of sexual pleasure, thus the mirrored self already refers to castration.[126] Aptly referencing Romantic fairytales, Dolar explains that the use of the double allows the subject to experience keen anxiety as the double ranges from a hallucination that he can only see or a shadow or split part of the subject that allows for all the double to break the rules and commits illicit acts that the subject receives blame for. Since the desired object is only a hindrance to the subject's experience of jouissance, the desired object is never the real goal, only a pathway to the real goal.[127] Due to the double's close proximity, in *Mysterier* Minutten has Nagel's missing jouissance. Several instances after Nagel's failed attempts with Dagny, then Martha, he speaks to Minutten and invites him to listen to him, though only to give him his long monologues and confessions.

The dream relates to the fairytale of the Lykteman's daughter because the Lykteman poses a similar threat to the connection between Nagel and his daughter similar to the threat that Minutten poses to Nagel in his dream. Hamsun writes Nagel's confession of the dream twice, once directed at Dagny early in the novel, and the other at Minutten, when he admits in anger that Minutten is the only one who truly knows him.

At the same night when Nagel tells his fairytale, he mentions a dream he has of Minutten. When he initially describes his dream to the women at the party, he portrays how Minutten pursues him through an open moor with tree roots lying everywhere. A few details alarm the reader of this strange interaction. One involves the description of the tree roots like "underlig forvridde ormer"[128] [strange twisted worms] that stymied his progress to get to Nagel. Another related detail is that Nagel gets closer to him when he taunts him and leaves his hiding place from behind the rock, yet Minutten cannot find Nagel until he grabs his hand. Once he does so, Minutten is able to leave the marsh and enter the hiding place of the rock. Nagel himself recounts in the following way: "Vi gik ut av myren, trærøttene var ham ikke længer til noget mén da han hadde fåt tak i handen min, og vi kom til stenen der jeg først hadde skjult mig…"[129] [We walked out of the marsh, the tree roots were no longer of any use to him once he'd gotten hold of my hand, and we came to the rock where I had at first been hiding].

The marsh land with tree roots gives Nagel the advantage, as he seems imperceptible, like a ghost. Only when Minutten can sense him is Nagel caught. During the chase, Nagel notes how he can see Minutten despite the distance and hear his groans and perceive Minutten's eyes "fulde av lidelse"[130] [full of suffering]. While the dream itself is not related to the fairytale, it sets up the friction between the characters. Later when Nagel confronts Minutten of his dream of him, he even suggests that the town considers how Minutten conveys a favorable and innocent reputation, yet Nagel claims to know his real identity and exposes two incidents of how Minutten presented obstacles to Nagel.

If a reader considers the function of the Lyktemann in the fairytale, she considers how it depicts the danger of the Lyktemann as having those strange eyes that peer at him, just as Minutten also examines Nagel. The figure, the Lyktemann—Jack-o'-lantern in the English translation—peers at Nagel with uncanny eyes, hinting at the fact that the gaze is familiar to Nagel as Minutten looks at him in a similar way. According to Kittang, the Lykteman symbolizes the father in the triangular structure that characterizes much of the love relationships in Hamsun's early writing. Kittang explains that the Lyktemann initially invites Nagel to the tower, and he only turns evil once his daughter becomes involved with Nagel.[131] Lyktemann fights Nagel for his daughter's purity, as he is aware that Nagel perceives her—and by extension, Dagny—in an erotic way, thus his uncanny gaze shows the struggle for power.[132] Minutten's obstacle in Nagel's pursuit of Martha and his own suicide parallel the Lykteman's power in prevailing over Nagel's bond over the blind daughter. Since Nagel provides this struggle in his fairytale, he unknowingly accepts Minutten's role in providing an obstruction to his goal; it is one paradox that he cannot escape due to Minutten's connection to Nagel's identity. Since they are connected through each other's identity—Minutten is Nagel's double, Nagel unknowingly puts him in the fairytale symbolized through the Lyktemann's character.

While Minutten is not a focal point in this discussion, his presence in the novel functions similarly to the way that Nagel narrates his frustration with Lyktemann. The polarities between Lyktemann's daughter's beauty and artistry and Lyktemann's brutality show the inner struggle within

Nagel. Lyktemann's victory demonstrates the fact that Nagel could not allow his better version of himself to win. Minutten prevents Nagel from getting close to Martha, the later crush after Nagel moves on from Dagny. More importantly, he empties Nagel's flask of acid and prevents him from going through his suicide, thus blocking Nagel from his own attempts to end his life. In other words, he robs him of his choice to end his life as Lyktemann threatened Nagel from seeing his daughter again.

Nagel's strange outbursts, as beautiful and vivid as they may be, indicates a lack of self-awareness. In Jørgen Elbek's examination of Hamsun's early work during the 1890s, he asserts that *Mysterier* shows the inner psyche of a man's troubled perspective,[133] thus explaining for the way that different characters represent parts of a person's mind. Citing *Pan* as the story of love and Nature, Elbek describes this work as referent to the Symbolist movement and *Mysterier* as showing the psyche.[134] According to Michal Kruszelnicki, many writers have posited that Nagel does not know himself. Kruszelnicki notes Rolf N. Nettum's study of Nagel as a person who attempts to communicate the mythological connection between all living matter through his sensation with nature and stories, but cannot render this task successfully.[135]

By doing so, Nagel presents how he uses symbols to fabricate a reality, thus concealing his true identity—death in the sense that he stifles his true preoccupations and suicide. On the one hand, this fairytale functions as an expression of Nagel's desire to attain the power of Lyktemann's daughter and her world of beauty, hence surpassing humanity and human limitations. Both interpretations pertain to the idea of the fairytale as an ellipse in psychoanalytic speech, in which it interrupts the main flow of the narrative, to convey the symbolic meaning of female power over a man's fragile humanity. The rupture between being and meaning breaks further when Nagel loses hope and fails to convince himself of his myth, thus leaving the narrative as mysteriously as he came into it.

The fairytale foreshadows his impending death, while simultaneously showing the myth that failed to be. Adding to the drastic nature of his fate, Nagel believes his ring gave him power but succumbs to his own destruction when he loses it. When Nagel drops his ring and drinks the flask, he decides to commit suicide, yet by coincidence, he does not die as he intends yet dies due to the fact that he lost the ring. In so far as the ring functions as his last shred of evidence for his belief in his myth, the coincidence here is that Nagel considers death but has thoughts that he isn't going to die. Furthermore, it is also a coincidence that Nagel dies in pursuit of the ring when he does jump into the water and never rises again. Prior to Nagel's death, Nagel experiences doubt in his ability to believe in his myth, as his last conversations with Minutten serves as evidence for this failure. His double brought him his death, as he failed to believe in his own myth. The failure of the symbolic, as in the death of Nagel as myth, coincides with his real death. Apt in Nagel's real death, he loses his ring, the symbol of his mythical existence, and drowns in pursuit of it. He drowns in the river looking after it, resulting in a loss of his self-belief but also an inability to overcome his failures.

Illustration: The Tower

Chapter 4

What Remains Omitted

During those early years of my investigation, I revealed my vulnerability to a mixed audience of Norwegian and American scholars, thinking that it would prove my intent to become a scholar in Norwegian literature. Right before I gave my talk, I listened to my friend's presentation on a Swedish textile artist. Though I tried to focus on his words, as any supportive friend would, I felt the mixed sensation of anticipation of my own presentation with my own feelings of admiration for the topic that I had selected. As I sat in the chair in an audience of others, I experienced the sensation of sitting in proximity to an enclosed fire. Though the room was air-conditioned, I removed my jacket due to the heat. As I reflected over the words of my presentation, I explained to myself that I was feeling a new kind of nervousness that combines a love for the topic with an uncertainty of how others would perceive this affection constructed through psychoanalytic thought.

By the time I had to present, I was on a panel of Norwegian scholars. When I started speaking, my voice eased into a soft breath, especially when I pronounced the Norwegian text that I had little knowledge of. The topic of eros in the forest transported me there, reducing that harsh tone I usually use into a breathy voice more akin to how I read my paper to myself in an enclosed room. I looked at the audience from time to time and tried to not let their stares detract me from my eccentric reading of *Pan* and *Victoria*. Afterwards, I went to the bathroom to pad a cold towelette on my skin, and I looked in the mirror and had never seen such a violent tinge of orange and red streaks across my cheeks. In the span of 20 minutes during my talk, I regained my youthful glow.

Paulo Coelho, in *The Alchemist*, portrays the wise words of a man to a boy about the lure of beginner's charm during his pursuit of his personal legend. When one first takes a risk to pursue their goals, they have little issues due to the fact that they need to get a taste for their journey before they realize larger risks. My beginner's luck surfaced through so many comments on my talk, a time when I did not know the Norwegian language. The luck lasted a few months after the conference when I taught during the summer. The sun burned particularly hot during that time, though the sensation paled in comparison to the moment that made me question the origin of the heat.

During the first days of class, I stood at the front of the room waiting for all the students to arrive. I had been writing a few instructions on the board when I heard the sound of rolled wheels stop abruptly followed by a sharp sound of a board on a floor and the door open. Turning on my heels, I picked up one of the syllabi to give to the student who had just walked in. From the corner of my eyes, I could see sneakers and the edge of a skateboard. I looked up and accidentally touched the hand of a student who took the syllabus from me. I looked into his blue eyes and stepped back, as he smiled and nodded in acknowledgement. A jolt of electricity from our contact made me jump back, and I wondered if it meant that his insights would enlighten the future class discussions.

Months later I realized the source of the jolt—the fire had transformed into an electric spark.

Sometime before the conference, I had a dream where a man in sepia had kissed me at a train station. I had been hat-shopping at a little cart with my sister. Yet, I wandered to look at the train station. The train was off at a distance in the sunlight. I walked closer to it to inspect if it was a train from the past or streamliner. I recall someone touching my hand, making me turn toward the person. I saw a tall young man with a head full of hair that shined blond and red but was chestnut brown at the roots. He wore a pince-nez that reflected the glare from the sunlight and a long brown overcoat with matching slacks that hung on him, as if it were slightly larger. He pulled me toward him to kiss him before walking into a crowd of people. Once I recovered myself—my breath left me—I ran toward my sister to tell her of the man who had kissed me, a man who was familiar to me though I had only begun to see him before awaking. The glint from the sunlight reflected from his eye glasses shielded his eye color to me as he pulled away from me.

I regained my breath once I awoke from the sun's rays. After a series of similar dreams with this man in sepia, I recognized the pattern. Instead of writing about the sensation of these dreams right after I awoke, I composed an email to a mentor about a logical explanation to these dreams. I expected a response on Sigmund Freud's notion of dreams as wish-fulfillment, as even I knew that I longed to be the next up and coming scholar on nineteenth century Norwegian literature, particularly a Hamsun scholar. A possible source was the dream of a meeting someone at the train station could illustrate my own desires to embark on a new research opportunity overseas.

My mentor's emailed response, however, made me stare at the computer screen in longer than usual.

In *Specters of Marx,* Jacques Derrida defines the specter as "a paradoxical incorporation, the becoming body, a certain phenomenal and carnal from of the spirit."[136] Inherent in his definition, Derrida mentions the contradiction within the specter as an entity that transgresses the incorporeal and the carnal, prompting the living person to take a particular course of action. Basing his analysis on Shakespeare's play *Hamlet*, Derrida defines the specter as "neither soul nor body, and both one and the other."[137] Furthermore, Derrida's notion of the specter demonstrates that specters manifest themselves as visible beings though they are meant to be invisible. In regard to Marx, he further compares it to the spirit of Marx's work, The German Ideology, as "a supernatural and paradoxical phenomenality, the furtive and ungraspable visibility of the invisible."[138] In this comparison, he briefly mentions the exchange value as representing an object that is not physically present and stands for something else, or possibility for a new system that takes over the former. Instead of taking this direction to answer my questions, I look to Derrida's metaphor of a ghost other as light, but a form of light that provokes the subject to figure out an intended message. He states,

> This flow of light which captures or possesses me, invests me, invades me, or envelops me is not a ray of light, but the source of a possible view: from the point of view of the other...It is because there is something other that watches or concerns me. This Thing is the other insofar as it was already there—before me—ahead of

me, beating me to it, I who am before it, I who am because of owing to it.[139]

He attributes a competitive aspect to this specter in relation to the subject. By indicating that the specter is an entity that lives prior to the subject, Derrida infers that the specter from the position of the other has an advantage of life experience and knowledge of death. In doing so, the specter can look at the subject in a way that the subject cannot. In this perspective the specter takes on a certain vantage point, one apart from the subject to better grasp the subject's subjectivity. Although Derrida clarifies by indicating that the specter is not light, he describes it as a flow of light with a sense of perception. This specter proves its superiority since it knows the subject's path, as it beats the subject to the destination prior to the subject's knowledge of it. For this reason, Colin Davis refers to the specter's gaze as a type of higher being as "the Other as pure, commanding alterity."[140] In this respect, the specter takes on a ghostlike essence, a presence of an absence that perceives the subject with a more informed perspective than that the subject has of herself.

This presence addresses a researcher's quest for learning more about an author's motives for writing the work. Yet, its power as a commanding alterity makes me consider whether the researcher has written something that disturbs the alterity that harkens its presence. Or is it the opposite? Does the researcher write content that makes the writer address the researcher as a way to beckon them more to the true motive of their writing? If the researcher has experience as an artist with all the accompanying moods and dispositions, does the writer then request that researcher's particular attention? I think so, as it is the only advantage I have to feel for the writer's work, a mirroring of habits and moods.

A year before a strong fog disrupted our means of traveling, I continued working on another conference paper that involved my analysis of a man's mysterious entrance into a northern Norwegian village. In one particular dialogue, a man told a woman what he admires about the difference between the Norwegian huldre and the beliefs of other cultures. He mentioned that the direction of the sun affects the way people think and their customary diets. While I wrote about the way that this man attempted to use his identity as a myth, I did not address the way that this dialogue resonated within me. Instead, I internalized it and addressed it in a dream.

I was in an unknown yet familiar city, as I knew my way around it. For example, I knew that a particular sandwich shop was two blocks west from where I walked just as I knew that I would need to take a cab to the post office. The city center was cleaner than Los Angeles and had a central park in the form of a square. A series of buildings framed the park. Although I had never seen this city before, I had the same feeling that I once had in my early twenties when I walked around Westwood during the late 1990s. All of a sudden, I saw a short Latino rushing toward me. Once he saw me, he ran toward me, moving past groups of people. Although I didn't recognize him, he too was familiar to me. I expressed this sentiment through the Norwegian phrasing of the sentence: Han var kjent. As I was learning Norwegian, I spoke of my perspective of that as a nonnative Norwegian speaker. One could express "I know it" as "Jeg vet det" or "Jeg kjenner det." The word "kjenner" means "to know," and it also has the context of being known such as the word "kjent" or a celebrity as in "en kjendis." "Kjenner" can also mean "to feel," thus the context of someone being familiar to me was better expressed in Norwegian than in English. Han var kjent for meg. He was familiar to me, but in a sense that this familiarity was based on a feeling rather than a recognition based purely on sight.

He was dressed in warm clothing, a plaid shirt and jeans. When he stood before me, he took off his hat as a means of respect and said, "Por favor, el señor tiene un mensaje." Initially, I stammered and replied that he was mistaken. I excused myself and kept walking briskly, as a woman never knows when or how her safety might be jeopardized.

He then tried to stop me by moving in front of me. He held his hat in his hands. There was a faint look in his eye, the way that the eyelashes touched the folded eyelid, that seemed like I had seen it before, like in the expressions of my ancestors that I had seen in my maternal grandma's photo album—he was my great-grandfather, Herman.

Perhaps it was this familiarity that made me stop to listen to him. I followed him up to an old building with columns. Seeing that we walked into a library we rushed inside, I stopped feeling as if he would threaten me, as nothing could happen in a library. At least, I felt this way at that moment we passed by the columns and walked straight into the building.

He led me into a large room with a man sitting at a desk. He had his chair facing the wall behind him. Upon hearing my entry, he turned around quickly. My eyes scanned the place. The walls surrounding us were filled with books from wall to ceiling—a researcher's paradise. My gaze fell back onto an older gentleman who wore a suit and sat behind a desk. This man and this desk faced me with the stack of neatly arranged books as his backdrop. He did not say a word, but only gave me a knowing smile. In regard to this older man, the Norwegian phrase denoting recognition fit my sense of familiarity, this time based on sight. Since I recognized him as the older version of the man in sepia, I would say "Jeg kjenner ham igjen" or "I recognize him/I know him again." Instead of the wide-eyed stare and faint flush of rose in his cheeks present in the younger version, I knew him again through that faint glint in his eyes, though he looked at me with distanced acceptance—the way a person regards a subject of study that no longer elicits wonder and awe but more knowledge of what made that subject appear mysterious.

I stared at the man whose smile widened with a sense of taunting, as if he had uncovered something that I kept hidden. I started raising my voice, shouting "How dare you scare a poor man just to get to me? Why didn't you just tell me anyway?" Yet, the man sat behind the desk with a knowing smile and did not answer.

I awoke with the sight of the man in the library still fresh in my mind along with the repeated words, "El Señor tiene un mensaje, El Señor tiene un mensaje, El Señor tiene un mensaje, El Señor tiene un mensaje." Though my great-grandfather Herman was summoned to deliver a message to me, I never heard the message itself. Before I could even state the possible messages, I had to accept that the lack of a message was a sign itself. The message was never meant to be delivered, only the lack of acknowledgement on a matter that I did not think mattered. Possible source of dream: The day before I reviewed Roland Barthes's essay "Myth as a Semiological System," in particular, his section on the second-order signification process. I looked over the signification process to describe

Nagel's coded message in his monologue to Dagny in Hamsun's second novel *Mysterier*.

<table>
<tr><td>1. Signifier Roses</td><td>2. Signified Love</td><td></td></tr>
<tr><td colspan="2">3. Sign (Passion for a person)
I Signifier</td><td>II Signified</td></tr>
<tr><td colspan="3">III Sign (Signification)</td></tr>
</table>

4.1 Barthes' chart[141]

<table>
<tr><td>1. Signifier</td><td>2. Signified</td><td></td></tr>
<tr><td colspan="2">3. Sign
I Signifier
Passion for a person</td><td>II Signified
Form of roses in photography or painting</td></tr>
<tr><td colspan="3">III Sign (Signification)
Passion identified but concealed/the properties demonstrated in particular art form</td></tr>
</table>

4.2 Barthes' chart with Lisa's Explanations of Barthes Second Order System (Myth)

A part of my text, later to be redacted in future edits of this conference paper, mentioned the second-order signification process in which the original signifier and signified become the sign in myth. Roland Barthes defines myth as "a mode of signification, a form..."[142] Prior to his explanation of myth as a second order signification process, Barthes breaks down the idea of signifier leading to the signified, or the concept, and the sign, the correlation between the two terms. Giving the examples of roses as a signifier for the concept of passion, Barthes gives a basic understanding of the common use of language.[143] He also attributes meaning to sign, so that one understands the ways by which the form of the signifier gives shape to the concept, the signified, in order to produce meaning. Such meaning, however, appears figurative, as in the case of the roses equating love. In myth, the language order still follows the signifier + signified = sign equation, but the signifier in myth already has first sign. For this reason, Barthes calls the language in myth a second order signification. In myth, the signifier already contains the "signifier + signified= sign" equation, which has a particular meaning and history. While the signified in myth does distort the original meaning embedded in the signifier, the signification process in myth "naturalizes" or makes the meaning in question natural and appear reasonable.[144]

For Barthes, his understanding of the sign in reference to the dream is the "functional union" of the dream content and the manifest meaning, or the behavior of the person recalling the dream. But upon more introspection in mythology, a dreamer's intention in behavior is the actual signified in the second-order signification process.[145] Since I had read and reread the text many times but failed to mention Barthes' use of Freudian ideas, I understood that the message redacted in the dream was in fact the overlooked text. My intention to leave out a certain part of my heritage when presenting on this literature reflected my initial response that I had when I first read that part in *Mysterier* when I questioned Nagel's omission of a cultures who were regarded as people of the sun. I never asked the question that I had initially thought and forgot until my unconscious prompted me to see the man whom I took as my maternal great-grandfather deliver a message that was not there. This omission mirrored the one I consciously made when I was analyzing Barthes' second-order signification process and removed it from the final edits of the essay. In short, Nagel's omission of a range of cultures made me repress my own question which then resurfaced in a dream where a message is never uttered. As I reworked my conference paper and turned it into a longer essay, I omitted the part on Barthes' second-order signification process involved in mythology.

The same mentor who had emailed me the suggestion on specters had once expressed concern that factoring in identity in one's analysis might weaken the work, a claim that I agreed with. The French thinkers I reference, however, felt so natural and common sense to me, as if their thoughts permeated my own. Though the different French thinkers often obfuscate their meaning with analogies, metaphors and abstract terms. I do the same in my writing and often work hard at clarifying my intended meaning from the interpretations readers might get from my abstract terminology. I get lost when I explain the brilliance of their concepts and then articulating my use of their terms; when I do so, I only wish to express how seamlessly their words inform my mindset. In some dreams, I often start speaking in French when I first see the older Norwegian writers. When I overhear my unconscious speaking words I have not uttered for a while, I marvel in happiness that I retained it.

Yet, later I stated my concern about presenting my work as an American to a European audience, mainly filled with Norwegians. When I texted my sister my concern over appearing too weak as a scholar due to a lack of many years of scholarship in the area in combination with my beginner's level in the Norwegian language, she had responded that I had the benefit of having a Latina background. I read and reread the text in confusion – but what did that background have to do with studying Norwegian literature? Without much thought, I had texted that it had nothing to do with the Hamsun's work and the Hamsunian male that I was analyzing. I shut down the conversation.

In light of interpretations, I consider Cathy Caruth's work, *Unclaimed Experience*, that has her discussion of Lacan's reinterpretation of Freud's discussion of the father's dream of the burning child. Caruth explains how this dream shows the father's responsibility of parenthood becomes disrupted through his wish to continue dreaming. She states, "The bond to the child, the sense of responsibility, is in its essence tied to the impossibility of recognizing the child in its potential death."[146] Caruth poignantly suggests that the father's dream places him in a bind to keep dreaming to see his child survive from the fire or to wake up to become aware that his child is really burning. Either way, the father wishes to see that the child really lives, only to be disappointed in the reality of his death. Though Caruth speaks of trauma, while the scholars on hauntology refer to the presence of a perceiving other, I consider Derrida's original inspiration of having Hamlet's father appear to Hamlet and its ensuing familial trauma. Both perspectives consider the importance of family, especially in the case of Hamlet's father where such knowledge penetrates Hamlet's life mission and interrupts his plans for himself. The experiences of one's family often intertwine with the life mission one chooses to take regardless of how explicit one expresses the impact of familial influence. In my case, the latent meaning—Barthes' term for the real meaning of the dream—of the omitted message gains more significance when I consider my intention to hold back from expressing my initial thoughts of that magical scene in *Mysterier*.

In the first order of signifier and signified, the signifier are the words of my great-grandfather, "El Senor tiene un mensaje [the man has a message]," which leads to the signified of the older man's smile and knowing glance and a lack of message. In the second order signification process, this dream becomes a new signifier, which French thinkers can agree that lead to different signifieds. One signified that I am examining is the combination of the omission of my reaction to my sister's words that reminded me of my ethnicity and the omission of Barthes' explanation, which reminded me of my values. Both form a unique combination in my heritage—one defines the cultural background that I was born into, while the other alludes to my choice of cultural values. Due to the omission of a culture in a form of literature that I felt a compulsion to analyze, I left out Barthes to fit in more psychoanalytical information on sublimation, namely in Lacan's tradition.

Expanding on Derrida's idea of the specter, Davis suggests that the specter presents an opportunity to explore certain liminal boundaries of the living and the dead, perhaps between the writer researched and the writer doing the researching. When he expresses the exploration of ghosts as "push[ing] at the boundaries of language and thought,"[147] I consider the ways that another examination of a text, in particular about the supernatural itself, garners closer study, especially if an analyst is taking an alternative method.

In terms of the need for other interpretations of older literature, Jeffrey Andrew Weinstock states that the specter's liminal position demonstrates resistance toward binary structures, hence taking on significance in the deconstructive method. In particular, when he refers to the ghost as "neither living nor dead, present or absent," he also shows how one cannot define it as belonging in one category.[148] More than just a metaphor for additional literary interpretations, the spectral turn that Weinstock mentions affirms the need for multiple interpretations of stories and characters, particularly ones that are accepted in classical interpretations, or in my case, affirming interpretations based on aesthetics. In a similar focus on interpretation, Julian Wolfreys examines nuance in text as a form of haunting in the sense that the text presents a limit between the living and the dead due to the reader's interpretation of different aspects of literature that may differ from the writer's intention.[149] Since the definition is broad and assumes that any text presents a ghostly presence that beckons readers and analysts to reexamine the work, it presents an issue when trying to consider an author's purpose. Both Wolfreys and Weinstock refer to the multiplicities in interpretation, much like the ethereal qualities of ghosts. In presenting the notion of ghosts as interpretation of text, the scholars consider the possibility of multiple readings as having a presence of the original text analyzed.

Thus, in the context of literary research, scholars hint at this wonderful meeting of two minds through the plurality of interpretation. As Todorov mentions in his explanation of the fantastic, one must suspend their doubt of the supernatural as a means of figurative expression in order to judge a work as such. A researcher can, however, hold both beliefs—one in the supernatural, the other in reason—to engage in the total view of a work of literary art if the work uses aspects of the supernatural. To uphold both views, one writes in one method and explicates using literary analysis to explore the logical interpretation of the wonderful resonance within literature. Yet, the other view, the more esoteric one, would entail an ability to abandon such ideas to honestly see how the work affects one's ability to reason, thus building on the aesthetic that the writer starts and the researcher continues.

In context of my own heritage, if I uphold the view that Great-Grandfather Herman came to send me to a man whose smile reminded me of information I knew, I need to remember that I overlook an important fact. I used to believe that Hamsun's oversight of naming the cultures of people of the sun implied that I was not able to partake in the growing community of scholars. Yet, the opposite is also true. If a cultural background is not mentioned In regard to a discussion that seems to invite my participation, then the information was omitted for my entry—I hold the message.

Illustration: Transitional Space

Chapter 5

Art Manifests as Humans

In an earlier chapter, I discuss a Lacanian perspective on sublimation to explain for the way that Glahn transforms his desire for Iselin and the forest and starts to emulate her behavior, thus inferring a change in his identity. This portrayal illustrates the way that sublimation changes not only the object of desire but the subject as well. Within this discussion, I include Johannes's withdrawal from society and his disappointment over love to show how his seclusion into creativity changes the way he perceives reality. Furthermore, in another chapter, I discuss Nagel and his creative storytelling as a form of art to lure Dagny. In this case, Nagel portrays his wish to become a mythological creature from the forest and sublimates this desire in the creation of the story that he uses to get Dagny's attention. Nagel's creativity depicts brilliance, yet it also reveals a hidden preoccupation with death.

In all of these examples of sublimation, Hamsun demonstrates how the creative energy changes the male protagonist and empowers the female supernatural being. It is significant to note that these female characters are not significant characters in the entire novels, yet they shift the behavior of the male protagonists. By doing so, these often-overlooked women elicit a new perspective on their significance.

In the next discussions of sublimated love and affection, I examine three different instances that involve main female characters who inspire male artists to use art as a means to depict their feelings for the women. While Hamsun's respective portrayals of sublimation reveal a shift in the men's identities and focus on men's creative behavior, these upcoming narratives more strictly portray the role of art. For two examples, the men sublimate their feelings for the women and use to depict their likeness in stone. In the final discussion, the narrator shows a complicated approach, as he depicts his feelings in an article where he evaluates a painter's depiction of a mythological woman. Yet, instead of being the final point of his sublimation, the narrator meets a woman who resembles the woman in the painting. Thus, the examples of women's likeness in statues differ, as the male artists worked on their art as a sacrifice for their inabilities to consummate their feelings for the women. In the example of the narrator who writes his article, his feelings of admiration are for the mythological woman as she is portrayed in paint and then through his analysis. Thus, his fortunate encounter with a woman who bears his likeness raises his expectations to successfully develop a relationship with her. Thus, when art becomes the central result of sublimation, the art piece itself exposes secrets from the characters, as if the art piece itself becomes infused with life. Unlike the examples of sublimation in the previous chapters, Henrik Ibsen's *Når Vi Døde Vågner* [*When We Dead Awaken],* Sigbjørn Obstfelder's *Korset*, and Knut Hamsun's "Dronningen av Saba" reinforce how certain art works reveal the inherent secrets within the main characters that the characters wanted to shield yet exposed without their conscious awareness.

To briefly summarize "Dronningen av Saba," a narrator tells his event of having met a woman during his travels to Sweden. This woman gives him her hotel room when she overhears that he needs a room but doesn't intend to give him more than her kindness. The narrator, however, takes it as a sign of her interest and recalls her several years later when he continues to misinterpret her actions to the point where he follows her to Kalmar, Sweden. To give himself a reason to travel other than stalking her, he begins to purchase antiques. In Kalmar, he discovers she is engaged to someone, so he gives up his quest for her. By repeatedly framing his story as "Saa nær som denne sidste Gang har [han] aldrig været det"[150] [as close to this last time, he has never been] he shows his inability to properly judge her actions as he never came close to being with her. This summary captures the important details in the plot, yet the narrator's psychological fixation on the Swedish woman portrays an even more compelling layer to the story and shifts the plot into the background. The narrator's audience underlies his story, as he professes that he is telling the truth.

This narrator resembles Nagel in their similar way of connecting idealized supernatural women to mortal women and in their need to have credibility from others. This narrator, however, does not exhibit signs of a death wish that Nagel does, my discussion shows; the narrator only asks for belief in his originality in his writing, while Nagel creates beautiful imagery as the last attempt to hold onto life. For this reason, the discussion of "Dronningen av Saba" and *Mysterier* remain in separate chapters.

The narrator's fascination with the Swedish woman centers on the myth of the Queen of Sheba, as he compares her not only to the mythological Queen of Sheba but also to his own critique of Julius Kronberg's painting of this mythological queen. The narrator mentions his review of the painting and references it, so when he first sees the Swedish woman, he attributes the beauty of the Swedish woman and likens her to the Queen in Kronberg's painting. Moreover, his analysis of Kronberg's depiction of the Queen lulls him into a hypnotic state, as he conflates the Swedish woman with the painting and his analysis of this painting. In doing so, this example of sublimation shows the narrator's conflation of the actual pursuit of the Swedish woman and the pursuit of his artistic ideal.

A few scholars comment on this conflation of pursuits but also the choice of the mythological figure, the Queen as Sheba, as a Western man's desire. Buttry describes this story as the sensitive male writer's artistic pursuit and confrontation with a female character who accentuates his artistic pursuit. Despite the inability to conquer what he longs to pursue and resulting despair, the strained difficulty in the chase gives meaning to the narrator.[151] In other words, the pursuit for the artistic ideal leads to his ideal for the Swedish woman, as he feels that the spirit from the painting as synonymous to the woman. Her assessment of the story emphasizes the role of the artistic impulse and its impact on the narrator's psychological mindset. Another scholar, Ellen Rees, focuses on the way that the unnamed protagonist's inability makes sense of the Swedish landscape due to Hamsun's lack of knowledge about the Swedish small towns. Rees infers that the absurdity of the lack of recognition in the towns, despite the protagonist's claim that he is familiar with the land, contributes to the protagonist's lack of credibility.[152] This issue of credibility comes into question for the reader, since the narrator pleads that he tells an honorable portrayal of events. Such insistence refers to his insecurity or his unreliability as a narrator.

In Elisabeth Oxfeldt's book, *Nordic Orientialism*, she describes Freud's layers of sublimation and cites Peter Kierkegaard's discussion of sublimation in the story. For instance, Oxfeldt explains Kierkegaard's critique of the story as means of sublimating the Swedish woman and turning her into a muse for his writing, thus turning the mortal into a legendary figure. Oxfeldt furthers indicates that the narrator uses his high estimation of art to give himself satisfaction. This assessment coheres with the view of the narrator's admiration of *his* assessment of the painting, as opposed to the view that the woman manifests the Kronberg's version of the Queen of Sheba. The narrator would achieve libidinal energy through the exploration of the painting, despite knowing that it is only an illusion that masks the disappointment in reality.[153] This interpretation of sublimation requires an explanation of the myth as well as the description of Kronberg's painting. In "Orientalism, Decadence and Ekphrasis in Hamsun's "Dronningen av Saba" Oxfeld describes this sublimation as "the desired erotic object is fetishized and converted into a muse..."[154] Since it is the narrator's assessment of the woman's gaze that makes him fall for the Swedish woman, the focus of his attraction toward her is the woman's gaze. As Oxfeld mentions using Lacanian terms, she addresses the Swedish woman as "an objet petit a—a woman upon whom desire is projects..."[155] This gaze, furthermore, symbolizes his need for credibility for his analysis of the painting and his originality of his thoughts, which could bring him financial success. Through her gaze, she validates him, a point that alludes to the original purpose of the Queen of Sheba's visit.

In the original story of the Queen of Sheba, a queen visits King Solomon and seeks wisdom from his insights and confirmation of the grandeur of his palace. In the biblical account 1 Kings 10, the queen arrives in a large caravan and witnesses the wondrous sights in King Solomon's palace, some including the food on the table, the officials, the cupbearers, and the burnt offerings. In response to the sight of all his treasures, she expresses, "But I did not believe these things until I came and saw with my own eyes. Indeed, not even half was told me; in wisdom and wealth you have far exceeded the report I heard."[156] Inherent in her comment is the idea that she had been told about the splendor of King Solomon's palace and tales of his wisdom but required her own experience of both to believe the accounts.

Furthermore, she credits that King Solomon must have pleased Yahweh to have His goodness bestowed on King Solomon, thus attributing the power of the divine onto a human. She states "Praise be to the Lord, your God, who has delighted in your and placed you on the throne of Israel."[157] So, the issue of the story is that her witness of King Solomon and his home proved the validity of the reports, whose validity required proof. The key detail in this biblical story is that she herself states that she "saw with [her] own eyes," hence alluding to the act of gazing at the wealth. With her own perception, she accurately judged the degree of King Solomon's wisdom and wealth. The hearsay about King Solomon's wealth requires her credibility, just like the unnamed protagonist's story requires credibility from the reader. While no one describes the power of the mythical Queen of Sheba's gaze in the biblical story, she enacts the power through her motive to seek proof for the hearsay of King Solomon's wealth and health.

Kronberg's painting *Drottningen av Saba* represents the Queen and enacts her beauty and power in her looking away from the viewer to assess the value of Solomon's wealth. Oxfeldt credits the direction of the Queen's gaze as a way of erasing the separation between the world in the painting and the world of the viewer.[158] The painting shows a woman whose gaze is off to her left side, as if she looks at the statue of a lion. Holding a thin staff with one hand, she looks amused, showing a slight indication of a grin. The soldiers surrounding her provide distance as she descends down a few steps in a seemingly short flight of stairs. This distance denotes her power, as they provide the space for her to evaluate Solomon's possessions. To further a demonstration of her power Kronberg represents four figures in the foreground kneeling on the floor; three of the men bow in obeisance, while the dark-skinned female holds offerings on trays with both hands upraised. The Queen in the painting is dark-haired and wears a large white-feathered headdress. As she is the central figure in the painting, she holds herself proudly in stark contrast to others who bow their heads in reverence.

By identifying the woman as European looking, the narrator conveys that an exotic woman would make the gaze unknowable and less of a gesture that compels the European man, at least at the time, to relate to her. He also addresses her dark hair as concealed with the effect of the shimmering aspect of the silver diadem. His words about her eyes, however, shift the previous comments about the preference for the knowable European woman into disarray. By focusing on the fact that the eyes reveal the woman's Ethiopian origin and its power compels the viewer to perish, the narrator alludes to the power of her gaze, one that examines for proof of the value of a man's wealth. Some scholars might indicate that Hamsun wrongly aligns the exotic woman with stereotypical features such as unknowable or mysterious. Oxfeldt assesses that the unnamed narrator's perspective of the Ethiopian woman as European depicts a collapse of the East and West binary.[159] Furthermore, Oxfeldt also describes Hamsun's own critique of the painting, as he did review the work and also wrote about his review through the story. Basing the narrator's experience on his own review in *Dagblaget*, Hamsun frames the narrator's experience of Kronberg's queen as "min tabte Lykke"[160] [his lost happiness]. Furthermore, the narrator focuses on the woman's gaze as the main appeal.

Kronberg's painting offers an artistic interpretation of the biblical story by focusing on the queen instead of on King Solomon's wisdom and palace, thus emphasizing the queen's act of looking as opposed to the actual riches itself. This focus on the gaze references the biblical story where she expresses how she had to see with her own eyes. When the narrator writes his article about the woman in Kronberg's painting, he focuses on the woman's gaze by expressing the following words:

> Kun hendes Øjne har den mørke Farve som røber hendes Hjemstavn, det paa engang tunge og fyrige Blik som bringer Beskueren til at fare sammen. Man vil ikke glemme disse Øjne, man vil huske dem langt borte og møde dem igen i Drømme.[161]

> [Only her eyes have the dark color that reveals her hometown, that at once heavy and fiery gaze that brings the viewer to perish. One will not forget these eyes, one will remember them far away and meet them again in dreams].

The narrator focuses on the gaze in the painting and decides to write about the gaze and its passion in the figure in the painting. Initially indicating that the woman does not look Ethiopian but rather European with much time spent under the sun, the narrator portrays her as a woman he can relate to, since someone too exotic would threaten his sense of emotional security. The narrator does experience satisfaction from the painting, but the painting is itself a product of Kronberg's fascination with the biblical tale. The narrator correlates his feelings about the Queen of Sheba in the painting to his experience of the Swedish woman.

When the narrator perceives the Swedish woman, he incorporates the gaze of desired woman with the gaze of the Queen in the painting. For example, when the Swedish woman stands up in the carriage, she examines him before stepping down from the carriage after standing tall and proud as a queen. This look stuns the male character, and he is left speechless with amorous feelings. By his own admission of how he likes the detail in his writing about the eyes, he comments that he will refer to this woman as the Queen of Sheba. In the following chapter, when the male character sees her again, he notes that he perceives her studying him and examining him as he does to her. His gaze on her eyes, just like his perception of the Queen's gaze in the painting, inspires him to fixate on her. The Swedish woman's proud stance reflects the boldness of the Queen in both the biblical account and the painting, thus it compels the narrator to base his feelings about the Queen in the painting onto the Swedish woman. His actions in his pursuit for the Swedish woman have little to do with her, but more so, the projected views of the figure in Kronberg's painting onto her.

Whereas in the novels Hamsun develops the interconnection between the artistic pursuit and the amorous pursuit, he shows the way that these two pursuits confuse the male writer, or the man who wishes to assert a writer's identity. Hamsun uses this biblical account and reinserts into a late nineteenth century Scandinavian context to show King Solomon's response, one that differs from the certainty depicted in the biblical accounts. Just as Hamsun chooses to focus on the gaze as an identifier for the Queen, the narrator is Solomon's Norwegian counterpart. Stripped from wealth and palaces, this nineteenth century Solomon seeks credibility for his wisdom in his storytelling. As such, sublimation functions as a means to turn reality into an artform based on the myth.

Considering that the narrator also wishes for credibility and validation as a writer and as a potential male lover, he sublimates the love for Kronberg's version of the Queen of Sheba that he then chooses to portray in his praise of the painting in his assessment of it. Thus, the narrator's satisfaction in his writing process itself shows an additional layer of sublimation, as he admired the sublimated form of a mythological woman. The narrator's interest in the Swedish woman connects to his need for credibility but he attaches himself to her based on her likeness to the painting. One must clarify that the woman's similarity to the woman in the painting inverses the usual trend in traditional sublimation; one usually goes from affection to a real person to a transfer these feelings to an art form, yet the narrator has fondness for an artistic ideal before finding a mortal woman to be the recipient of his feelings. Yet, when examining the narrator's feelings for the woman as a concrete manifestation for his need for credibility and validation, a reader considers that the Swedish woman functions as a physical form of his symbolic desires. With her reciprocation, her fondness for him could eliminate the troubling effects of the accusation of plagiarism, need for recognition, his fondness for an artistic ideal, and his wish for validation. Due to the over prevalent symbolic nature of his desires, the narrator does not really like the woman since he does not perceive her as she is.

The Swedish woman does get away from Hamsun's narrator, as she is betrothed to another man, thus her refusal to engage with him asserts a particular power over him. Furthermore, Kronberg's depiction of the Queen of Sheba possesses the narrator and displays a type of supernatural hold over him. This latter form of power supersedes the Swedish woman's appeal, as the Queen's appeal is more abstract and idealized. Without a way to effectively express this attraction and make sense of it, the abstract nature of the Queen's appeal remains nefarious. Anyone can manifest this appeal but, ironically, also deflect it.

The Statue as Replacement for the Woman

In his novella, *Korset*, Obstfelder presents a love story filled with heartache about a woman who enchants different men and shares strong bond with the narrator despite his discovery of her genuine affections after her death. As Mary Kay Norseng writes of this novella, it is a story of a man who "experiences life more profoundly than ever before."[162] The male narrator does experience some epiphanies through his interactions with beautiful Rebekka as well as after he realizes her amorous past with other men. Nærup furthers that the emphasis of poetic sensibility as the narrator's main goal in his acquaintance with her. Only a true poet could use his many illusions as the honest portrayal of his acquaintance with her.[163] Though most of thc story, the male protagonist chronicles his heartbreaking affair with Rebekka and his friendship with artist, Bredo, who creates a sculpture in her likeness. Initially in his acquaintance with Bredo, the narrator notes his fondness for him and shares his newly formed friendship with Rebekka. Though readers find her nonchalant response to his announcement of his friendship to Bredo a bit suspicious, the narrator believes that they should meet. Once Bredo shows the narrator the statue of Rebekka, the narrator feels his inner world crumbling, as the statue presupposes Rebekka's acquaintance with Bredo.

When Bredo shows the protagonist the statue built on Rebekka's likeness, the protagonist immediately senses that Rebekka betrayed him due to the intimacy of how Bredo represents her. The protagonist feels as if her soul is in the statue, "så var der dog altid deri noget af hendes legemes sjæl, hendes lemmers melodi"[164] [so there was always therein some form of the soul, the melody of her limbs]. While a reader might attribute this likeness to Bredo's talent, she recalls that the narrator had previously commented that Bredo's previous sketches lacked the unique character of his statue based on Rebekka. He notes that Bredo's drawings were "halvt sammensmeltet blanding af påvirkning og vage forsøg på at finde frem mod et jeg, der endnu ikke var dukket rigt op af livets bad"[165] [a half-fused mixture of influence and vague attempts to find an ego that had not yet emerged richly from the bath of life]. The sculpture not only embodied Rebekka's essence, as the narrator notes the "melody of her limbs" and "some essence of the soul" but also demonstrates a breakthrough in Bredo's artistic abilities. Thus, Rebekka's power, her ability to inspire a man to create in her likeness and compel his ability to craft with her seduction, arises from her tendency to give herself so willingly.

The narrator reflects on her ability to perceive her surroundings deeply, a power that makes her inspire men around her to act accordingly. He states, "I naturen, i kunsten, i manden, i altet var det ét, hvrofra alt stråled ud og flød tilbage—det øie!"[166] [In nature, in art, in man, in everything, there was one from which everything radiated out and flowed back —that eye!] Her ability to mediate between Bredo and the narrator crushes the narrator particularly because he feels that both Bredo and Rebekka betrayed him. Since his initial meeting with Bredo, the narrator felt a similar sensibility within Bredo and Rebekka. After noting that Bredo knew the particulars of her body, the narrator mentions that Rebekka sees "var det hos Bredo og [ham] noget fælles, der gjorde, at vi så det same hos kvinden"[167] [something within Bredo and (him) in common that they saw the same within the woman]. Thus, through Bredo's representation of Rebekka, the narrator attributes her power as that which allows him to connect with Bredo. The power in her eye shows her influence attracted them to each other.

In the case of Bredo's statue of Rebekka, Bredo successfully renders the accuracy of her likeness to the point where the narrator discovers her infidelity to him. Yet, for Bredo, the statue manifests all his amorous feelings for Rebekka that he cannot express due to her love for the narrator. While Bredo provides his own explanation of his suffering according to his situation with Rebekka, the words apply directly to the narrator's fascination with her. Bredo mentions,

> Men Kanske må kunst betales. Kanske må det Promethesverk her i dødens rige at ville trænge ind i algudens eget tabernakel, — harmoniens hjem, — skabelsens mysterium,--kanske må det bødes med titanens smerte…og titanens...savn[168]

> [But maybe art has to be paid for. Perhaps the Prometheus' work here in the realm of death must need to penetrate god's own tabernacle, — the home of harmony, - the mystery of creation, — perhaps it must be punished with the titan's pain ... and the titan's ... lack].

For Bredo, his artistic inclination requires that he must long for the woman for the sake of art, as loss in love is part of art's mystery. Alluding to the mythological, Bredo suggests that the creation process is akin to the ability to create from the destruction or death of love in order to communicate effectively. While Bredo's words arise from his own drunken reflection of his loss of love, they aptly frame the way that one should regard both Rebekka's influence on Bredo and the narrator. Since the narrator notes how Bredo's art lacked originality before Rebekka's presence, the reader realizes that Bredo's love and loss of Rebekka made his art powerful almost like it added more to his ability to express himself. The narrator's love made Rebekka more inclined to be with the narrator, thus causing Bredo to lose her.

The mythology that Bredo alludes to in the act of creation shows how art misguides people into falling for the human versions of the image. In his conversation with the narrator, he stutters that he saw Rebekka in the park, though he does not address her by name. Through his admission, he reveals his passion for her as he describes her unique qualities, her manner of walking, her dress, her dark hair. Prior to his monologue where he describes her in the park, he mentions how she left him, and his stuttering matches the same despondency that the narrator feels.

The statue's likeness to Rebekka references mimesis, which Otto Reinert defines as the "replication of the world of sensory phenomena in words."[169] Considering the Platonic and Aristotelian ideas of mimesis, Reinert asserts that it involves interpretation of a dramatic performance, as it functions as a mirror to the audience. It involves the audience members to use their intellect, as they consider the moral issues portrayed in art as a way to reflect on their experiences. As indicated in Robert Spoo's assessment of how art murders in order to create, art allows for many to reflect on their individual experiences despite the fact that the artist generalizes their representation of the human experience to a wide audience.[170]

Reinert's assessment of the artist's function is similar to Bredo's hopes in rendering Rebekka's beauty. He writes,

> The artist figures forth (represents, expresses, imitates) something within. How it all got there nobody knows, but there it all is—facts, imaginary facts, memories, obsessions, traumas, ideals, nightmares, visions, repressions, and the dread that nothing makes any sense. To communicate something vital to others is the artist's goal. And all that can be communicated is first in the mind[171].

This realization causes both men pain, as they realize that they love the same woman. While Obstfelder does not make clear as to whether Bredo sublimates his love for Rebekka, the statue captures Rebekka's essence and show a level of intimacy that causes grief to the narrator. Yet, in this case, art does not murder the individuality in the mortal woman, as it's the strong similarity in likeness and spiritual essence within Rebekka that makes the narrator feel betrayed. Though neither he nor Bredo never mention whether they have been intimate with Rebekka, the statue's similarity to Rebekka suggests that Bredo did establish some intimacy as he created a beautiful statue with her soul's essence despite his otherwise lackluster artistic abilities.

In regard to sublimation, Obstfelder's novella shows how both men connect Rebekka's sublime essence to Bredo's depictions of her. He uses his creation of art as a replacement for his lack of consummation with Rebekka. She does not reciprocate his feelings for her, as her confrontation about her true sentiments are addressed to the narrator. For this reason, Bredo has no other option but to transfer his feelings for Rebekka onto his artistic abilities. Through the act of creation, Bredo fulfills his purpose, yet his creation betrays him.

Consequently, Bredo's creation also evokes passionate feelings within the narrator, showing the way that art captures Rebekka's essence. As previously stated, Bredo's sculpture shows Bredo's feelings for Rebekka, but also a culmination of the narrator's feelings for Bredo and their connection. Since they first met, the narrator feels a close connection to Bredo in a way that seems more intimate than friendship but not erotic as his bond to Rebekka. When he meets Bredo, the narrator expresses excitement in their common sentiments shortly after stating that he is a sculptor. He states, "Jeg har vel neppe nogensinde havt slig pludselig lyst til at lære et menneske at kjende…også vi to til at samtale for os selv, vi gled bort fra de andre ved same bord"[172] [I have hardly ever had such an immediate desire to learn and know a human being… the two of us also came to talk to ourselves, we slipped away from the others at the same table]. Such a declaration shows a level of intimacy in terms of the conversations that he has with him. By expressing that he had not experienced such a desire to get to know someone, the narrator implies that Bredo's friendship excites him, as he wishes to know more.

In his acquaintance with him, the narrator notes his connection with Bredo to the point where he tells Rebekka about him. He says the following: "De mænd, jeg ellers i den tid var sammen med, havde jeg vel ikke fundet såmeget ved, at jeg havde føld denne higen. Det var anderledes med ham. Han havde gjort et sterkt indtryk på meg."[173] [The men I was otherwise with at the time, I had probably not found so much that I had felt this aspiration. It was different with him. He had made a strong impression on me.] Again, the narrator notes a particular longing for Bredo, hinting at Bredo's difference. His artistry makes him different from other men that the narrator knows, thus impressing him deeply with his philosophical insights but also the depth of his feelings.

Shortly after Rebekka tells him in a stern way not to ask her again, the narrator spends his time with Bredo. He confesses to the reader,

> Ialfald følte *jeg* den [en egen sympathi] for *ham*. Der var noget hos ham, som jeg ikke havde fundet ved andre, og som gav mig en fornemmelse af, at det jeg kunde føle, se og tænke, ikke var bare særheder, som ikke kunde være til hos andre end mig, med at det same kunde skjælve også i andre menneskers bryst, måske i nogen af de bedste, dem hvem livets music griber sterkest.[174]
>
> [Anyway, *I* felt it for *him*. There was something within him that I had not found in others, and that gave me a feeling that what I

> could feel, see and think were not just quirks that could not exist in anyone but me, but that the same could also tremble in other person's breast, perhaps in some of the best, those whom the music of life grips the strongest.]

This poetic phrasing captures the narrator's feelings about meeting a person with similar sensibilities, and it foreshadows the torture of the betrayal. Due to Bredo's similarity to the narrator, one implies that Bredo's connection to Rebekka manifests itself in his understanding of her soul as witnessed in the sculpture. Bredo could replace the narrator due to their similarities, thus supplanting him in the narrator's pursuit of Rebekka. Thus, the narrator's heartbreak occurs due to this understanding that Bredo offers Rebekka his artistry, an ability that the narrator cannot offer her. While the statue is only of Rebekka, not of Bredo himself, it addresses the secret connection between Bredo and the narrator as it symbolizes the connection between Bredo, Rebekka and the narrator. It references the excitement that the narrator feels about sharing his friendship with Rebekka, as the statue embodies the narrator's and Bredo's respective intimate moments with her; it manifests the aspects of her soul that the narrator proclaims as he examines it. Bredo's sublimated feelings evoke confusion for the narrator, as he perceives the admirable traits of Rebekka as he examines the statue, but also, he witnesses the statue as the result of a man's ability with poetic sensibilities. Therefore, he sees the product of a woman he admires from the man he admires.

The Statue as the Immortalized Woman

Taking place in a resort in the south of Norway, *Når Vi Døde Vågner* [*When We Dead Awaken*] focuses more on the backstory of the two characters, Rubek and Irene, and the psychological tension in their reunion. At a sky resort, Irene – clad in white – finds Rubek, whom she addresses informally, and confronts him on her feelings about his manipulation years prior when she was his model for his sculpture titled "The Resurrection." As soon as Irene walks across the stage, a reader perceives the way that she takes on attributes of the marble statue, as if she gained aspects of art despite being its human form. In Ibsen's initial description of Irene, he writes the stage direction as "en slank dame, klædt i fint, kremfarvet hvidt kashmir"[175] [a slender lady, dressed in fine, cream-white cashmere] and describes her with a pale face. Even Rubek's wife, Maja, describes Irene as "Skridende—som en marmorstøtte"[176] [striding—like a marble pillar], thus showing how Irene's identity shifts from one of mortality extending to the limits of immortality, as a sculpture is meant to do. In his discussion of James Joyce's thoughts on Ibsen's play, Robert Spoo describes the Irene's imagery as "the picture of a beautiful, shrouded corpse," a woman "with erect carriage and phantomlike demeanor,"[177] thus echoing the observation of Irene as a mortal woman who portrays aspects of the supernatural. Frode Helland furthers this observation by indicating how Irene compares to the statue by the fact that her movements are stiff while her facial expressions are empty.[178]

When they talk about the art-making process, Rubek describes the tension of feeling sensuous desire for Irene, but due to the necessity of creating art, he sublimates his desires for her in a traditional sense. The common understanding of traditional sublimation is that it entails the act of pushing aside earthly pleasures in order to portray such pleasures in a more abstract or spiritual way through an artform. He uses his feelings for Irene and channels them into his recreation of his image of her into a statue. Initially one perceives that Rubek cannot de-sublimate, or separate his desire for Irene from his enjoyment of her. He simply does not allow himself to enjoy her. Instead, he maintains his view of the sublime version of Irene and channels it through his statue, and as a result, he causes a loss of enjoyment for both himself and Irene. He chooses to desire the noble version of Irene and mandates that she do so as well, yet he also does not initially act on this desire for her.

Norwegian scholar Per Buvik writes of the sublimation in the drama in his article, "Kunstneren, Kjønnhet, og Kvinnen om Når Vi Døde Vågner." Buvik clarifies that through Irene's admission of Rubek's statue as their child, she infers how she experiences an erotic relationship with art. When she modeled for him, Rubek senses the erotic connection between them, yet Buvik claims that he "bestreber seg på å overskride, eller altrså subilmere, sin egen mannlighet"[179] [strives to transcend, or sublimate, his own masculinity]. Thus, Buvik contends that Rubek conflates the art and life as a form of sexuality.

Alena Zupančič, in her article "On Love as Comedy," explores Lacan's notion of sublimation as a process of ennobling the desired person to a higher deity and then the idea of sublimation as the goal of desire. Regarding the former explanation, I explored it in great detail in my chapter on Iselin, yet I examine Rubek's relationship with Irene as manifesting the latter explanation of sublimation. Zupančič explains that the sublimation allows for love to arise within a desirous moment, but only through a version of sublimation that she terms as "desublimation." She defines it as a "dislocation or de-centering of the sublime object in relation to the source of enjoyment."[180] Even though Zupančič then depicts love as that essence that allows us to make jouissance enjoyable, her definition of desublimation pertains mostly to the discussion of Rubek and his treatment of Irene. Her definition develops from Lacan's idea that the nature of the drive is similar to sublimation as the means of going beyond the object itself. This idea is similar to Copjec's notion of sublimation that allows drive as that which transforms the object, one that I briefly mentioned in my chapter on Iselin. As a result, desublimation gets rid of the inaccessible ideal that one places on a desired object to allow the person to experience jouissance for the person. While this notion offers a way for Rubek to pursue his feelings for Irene, he forgoes this option completely yet avoids transferring his feelings of admiration for his creation.

During his conversation with Irene, he recalls his previous admiration for her, thus showing proof of his earthly desires: "Og den overtro fyldte mig, at rørte jeg dig, begærte jeg dig i sanselighed, så vilde mit sind vanhelliges, så at jeg ikke kunde skabe færdigt det, som jeg stræbte efter"[181] [And the superstition filled me that if I touched you, if I desired you sensually, then my mind would be desecrated, so that I could not complete what I was striving for]. In his confession, he aptly shows how it was just a superstition in the art-making process that forced him to act on his desires for her. The statue itself was supposed to represent a woman who awakened from the dead, an awakening that Ibsen writes as "ædleste, reneste, idealeste kvinde, hun, som vågner"[182] [the noblest, purest, most ideal woman, she, who awakened]. By creating the statue in Irene's image, he takes his ideal of the woman as a "højere, friere, gladere egne"[183] [higher, freer, happier self] after her awakening from death as his truest desire. Rubek denies himself the love that he could have had with Irene, but to show further degree in the cruelty, he also robs Irene of her ability to express their desire. Hence, they embody traits of living humans, as they walk and talk and eat as most humans do, yet they lack an expression of love, an aspect that destroys their humanity.

In response to his confession, Irene mentions that she has died within, as she has given her soul to Rubek's sculpture in order to give life to it, thus forgoing her own mortal life. Despite the metaphorical nature of their discussion, Irene lacks humanity since she cannot give into her sensuality. In her conversation with Rubek about making a pilgrimage to the sculpture, she asks him, "Tror du kanske, jeg vilde død en gang til af det?"[184] [Do you think maybe I would die one more time from that?]. Her phrasing "one more time" denotes that she would have died a first time, which corresponds to her claim that she had previously given her soul to the sculpture and is dead. Although Irene's chooses to model for Rubek was for the sake of art, she endures a limbo-like state that robs her of enjoyment of living. For example, she marries multiple times, bears children, and models for other artists but results in killing them because she herself cannot offer life. To further the theme of her death, Irene models for a statue titled "The Resurrection," which includes an awakening from death. In the mythology of the sculpture, the figure manifests an awakening from humanity into a nobler state, a transfiguration that vitalizes the figure. In so far as Irene sacrifices her life for her "child," she switches roles and becomes the stature, a cold being that only represents life without feeling it.

When viewing Ibsen's plot twist in Irene's confrontation with Rubek, one perceives that sublimation helps reveal her power and hidden aspect of the artist's relationship with the model. Irene makes the choice to confront Rubek with her appearance of a ghostly statue come to life because this dramatic presence is the only way to awaken him, and perhaps herself. Her words define Rubek's life and critique his mission. When she utters, "Når vi døde vågner…Vi ser, at vi aldrig har levet"[185] [When we dead awaken, we see that we have never lived], she demonstrates that Rubek was successful in creating a powerful work of art, but she also critiques the project itself. Since the female pure figure resurrects from a deathlike sleep, in order to transfigure into a purer state, the female figure manifests a deathlike state. The theme of the sculpture mirrors the limbo states that both Irene and Rubek endure with the hopes that they can awaken, though Rubek's claim that Irene holds the key to unlock his heart suggests that he willingly believes in the possibility that he can awaken. In contrast to his optimism, Irene delivers her famous line to show that Rubek's awakening consists of the realization that he never truly lived, since he focused more on crafting the perfect idealized woman instead of seizing the opportunity to explore her with his senses.

Furthermore, she addresses him as an embodiment of a statue, "Din unge opstandne kvinde kan se hele livet ligge på ligstrå"[186] [Your young resurrected woman can see her whole life lying on a limb]. This claim changes the nature of Rubek's actions, causing him to become more passionate in his gestures and words. Through Irene's bold demeanor and confrontation, she enacts the sublime by addressing herself as "Din unge opstandne kvinde" [your young resurrected woman], and in doing so, Rubek accesses his passion for her. In addition to revealing irony in the plot development, Irene's actions empower herself, since she is restoring the humanity that was once lost.

In the act of desublimation, one decenters the noble aspects of the object to compartmentalize and allow for the person to experience jouissance. Yet, in this last encounter, Rubek and Irene do desublimate; instead of focusing on the banal aspects of each other, they only address the noble, thus pursuing each other as sublime people, the dead to die once again. The following interactions demonstrate how they perceive each other's sublime aspects and come back to life due to this process:

> Rubek: (slår armene voldsomt om hende): Så lad os to døde leve live ten eneste gang tilbunds—før vi går ned I vore grave igen!
>
> Irene: (henreven i lidenskab). Nej, nej,—op i lyset og i al den glitrende herlighed. Op til forjættelsens tinde![187]
>
> [Rubek: (slaps his arms violently around her): So let us two dead live for once--before we go down to our graves again!

Irene: (ravished in passion): No, no, up into the light and in all the glittering glory! Up to the mountain peak of promise!]

Although the terms “voldsomt” [violently] and “henreven i lidenskab” [ravished in passion] suggest more sensuous emotions, the words spoken address more sublime imagery of the dead dying again in the highest peak. Furthermore, Irene’s full agreement to follow him only occur after she feels transfigured. By definition, a transfigured being is one that has transformed into a more noble and beautiful person, and its religious connotation further makes use of the mountain peak to heighten its sublimity to an extreme. Thus, when considering Zupančič’s discussion, one perceives that Rubek and Irene do transform and decenter the banal and the sublime, yet they chose to acknowledge the sublime. This perception enables them to pursue each other, as desublimation would allow humans to do. As a result, Ibsen demonstrates that art has its destructive qualities, though more compelling to his point, art shifts one’s humanity as well as one’s perspective on attraction. Thus, through desublimation her transfigured allowed her to feel human to voice sensuous attraction but only by allowing themselves to voice each other’s attraction to each other as the living dead, supernatural beings or sublime beings.

Rubek’s sculpture, while not shown in the play, manifests itself indirectly through Irene’s presence and actions. Through her presence, one perceives the role of art as an entity that destroys life, but also restores it after humans confront their previous misdeeds with it. As previously stated, Irene and Rubek lose their humanity through the art-making process as a means of sacrifice, yet they quickly gain it as Irene embodies the statue itself. For this reason, sublimation here becomes a secondary process, more so an explanation for the way that art presents a duality of giving and taking away life from humans. Furthermore, the last confrontation reveals their previous fears in addressing their affections toward each other, thus having them experience the joy of rebirth.

Relevant to the pathos in the time of publication, this interpretation of rebirth refers to the trend in writing at the time. In Elinor Fuchs’s article “The Apocalyptic Ibsen: When We Dead Awaken,” Fuchs describes the climax moment as a moment of rebirth for both the “life-denying artist” and the "life-starved Irene" as they "advance ecstatically up…to an invisible peak beyond to consummate their spiritual union, reawakening to life…at the highest level of consciousness."[188] While Fuchs is clear to not entertain the Romantic notion of rebirth, she does reveal the way that this play written in the last year of the 1890s decade anticipates the apocalyptic pathos as the twentieth century. As opposed to reading notions of rebirth and transcendence in the statue, Fuchs aptly gestures the statue as "an allegory of conflict within the artist's soul,"[189] as the artist, Rubek combines the beastly depictions into his statues. Thus, Fuchs further explains that this combination of beast and human alludes to the battle between the "carnal and spiritual, earthly and heavenly, within each human soul."[190] In relation to my discussion, the statue's heavenly and earthly attributes relate to art's destructive and creative functions. Its duality ensures that the artist and model see the error in their assumption that the creative and heavenly pursuit allows for some release in their affections for each other. The statue's destructive and earthly function pertains more to their sacrifice, as the statue replaces the Irene's earthliness and therefore stores it within its marble body. Due to this focus on the sacrifice, Ibsen directs readers to examine the paradox of rebirth born from an unleashing of repression.

Spoo focuses his discussion on the way that art offers the male artist a way out of repressing his fears. When Irene addresses the statue as her child with Rubek, it "merges maternal and biological images with the more traditional aesthetic rhetoric of transcendence and immortality, hinting at the link between male fascination with the aestheticized female form and the fear and loathing inspired by the *unheimlich* maternal body."[191] Through Spoo's explanation of Freudian repression of the maternal body, he demonstrates Rubek's aim for his creation of his statue. Irene internalizes this goal and speaks of his statue as their child due to the fact that it took life from them. Spoo's explanation of attributing biological function to art-making implies a harmful quality in art-making. Attributing how it robs Irene and Rubek of their sensuality, the conception of the statue lacks the Romanticized view of art-making. Since the process of conceiving the statue killed the humanity within Irene and Rubek, art takes on a criminal function.

Spoo further captures the idea of art as a crime when he writes of the negative portrayal of how being a model for such a grandiose sculpture killed Irene. Spoo writes,

> Instead of giving her love, Rubek conferred on her an artistic immortality which spelled the death of her soul. The aesthetic act becomes an act of murder inasmuch as it must raze human individuality before it can rear its place a universalized art form. Art murders to create.[192]

In this assessment, Spoo confers the difference between human individuality, one gathered through the process of being mortal, and the universal content in art. Rubek transfers his emotions of lust for Irene in order to justify them in an artform. Furthermore, Spoo explains that such a crime of killing a mortal woman in order to immortalize her through art has its origin in repression of male fear of the maternal body. Yet, in Rubek's case, lustful feelings are not the only emotions he represses, as he cannot act on them due to his marriage with Maia. In his discussion of Freud and repression, Spoo mentions how men perceive the maternal body as an uncanny site, a place both familiar yet strange, because this body is simultaneously "a magical cave and a long-lost home."[193] Through the act of art, an artist transforms this repression into a desirable object, thus alluding to sublimation as a way to get out of repression. Thus, given this trajectory, the act of killing a woman entails a confrontation of the male artist with the maternal body, so it suggests that in the act of sublimation—at least in this context—the artist transforms the repressed fear into an object that he desires on a conscious level. By default, in the context of this theme of "art murders in order to create," it makes use of the crime and shows its detrimental side to humanity. For the sake of sacrifice, humanity is lost even though art reminds viewers of life's beauty.

In Rubek's discussion of his lust for Irene, he confesses that he must sacrifice them for the sake of his art, thus art spoils the experience of living. For other artists, however, the creation of a statue functions as the replacement for the desired woman. Thus, the act of immortalizing unrequited love leaves the model and artist unharmed in their humanity, save for the artist's longing for a woman who does not love him.

Yet, some scholars consider Irene's power as resistance against his power as an artist, thus showing the literary trends in the late nineteenth century. Helland aptly explains,

> I denne forstand ser Irene ut til å legemliggjøre en kritikk av kunsten i livets navn. Det ser ut til å ligge en motstand ot Rubeks prosjekt i selve gjenstandsmessigheten hos Irene; det at hun er natur, og slik objekt ffor hans blikk, konstituerer samtidig en motstand mot det livstømmende ved kunstnerens blikk.[194]
>
> [In this sense, Irene seems to embody a critique of art in the name of life. There seems to be a resistance to Rubek's project in Irene's objectivity itself; the fact that she is nature, and such an object for his gaze, constitutes at the same time an opposition to the life-draining nature of the artist's gaze].

In other words, Helland's assessment is that Irene's last actions in the play critique the function of art or the choice of art. This discussion of Ibsen's play serves as a conclusion to the portrayal of sublimation. In the other works, sublimation functions more as an alternative reality from the male character's mortal existence, or a psychological break from reality. Usually the women as objects are detached from the male character, either as figments of the character's imagination or an otherworldly source. In Ibsen's play, however, Irene's closeness to Rubek provides a different conclusion: It is this foreclosed relationship that Rubek sacrifices, thus showing how the choice for art supplants life with disastrous consequences.

Furthermore, Buvik's assessment about Rubek and happiness extends to the other men in the discussion, all sensitive and creative men who struggle with finding happiness in line with their artistic endeavors. Buvik states,

> Mennesket er ikke skapt for lykke, og den skapende (Rubek) og den følsomme (Irene) aller minst. Lykken, definer som et lykkelig forhold mellom mann og kvinne, kan bare bygges på illusjoner som alltid brister for kunsteren, den intellektuelle og den sensible.[195]

> [Man is not created for happiness, and the creative (Rubek) and the sensitive (Irene) least of all. Happiness, defined as a happy relationship between man and woman, can only be built on illusions that are always broken for the artist, the intellectual and the sensitive].

These words aptly capture the reason for the sadness in the men's struggle between their creative illusions and their pursuit for love. Only when they wish to conflate the two, do they experience hardships, as they feel they would have to choose only one. Buvik mentions the artist, the intellectual, and the sensitive, which describes the characters not only in this section but throughout the book. Such individuals cannot find happiness due to the nuanced observations of life that these traits entail for them to make. Much of the quest for find happiness while retaining creativity suggests that the writers bring in supernatural elements to bypass their tragic fate of unhappiness, thus imbuing characters such Iselin, Lyktemann's daughter, and Irene as those who are magical woman with powers that can relieve the mortal limitations. These supernatural women might make these men bypass the incompatibility of happiness when artistically inclined. Yet, the men experience a break from reality, removing the likelihood of attaining happiness. Furthermore, such a trend might reflect the artist and the muse theme that limits the woman's agency.

Beret Wicklund aptly expresses the literary trend of the artist and the muse and its seemingly equalizing of the genders, only to bring up a disappointing result for the muse. She states:

> Kvinnen har en suveren plass som den som beånder mannen og inngir ham inspirasjon, mens mannen er den som bearbeider inspirasjonen til et produkt. Han realiserer den ivirkelighetens verden. Musens rolle er dermed bade guddommelig og opphøyet, men den ligger samtidig utenfor den faktiske virkeligheten. Mannens dirking og idealisering av sin kvinnelige muse innebærer dermed at han samtidig holder henne fast i en posisjon utenfor realitetens verden. Dyrkelsen av kvinnen er dermed en form for undertrykkelse fordi hun fastholdes i en posisjon der hun ikke har innflytelse over hvordan hun blir brukt.[196]

> [The woman has a supreme place as the one who inspires the man and gives him inspiration, while the man is the one who processes the inspiration into a product. He realizes it in the world of reality. The muse's role is thus both divine and exalted, but at the same time it lies outside actual reality. The man's cultivation and idealization of his female muse thus means that he simultaneously keeps her firmly in a position outside the world of reality. The worship of women is thus a form of oppression because she is kept in a position where she has no influence over how she is used.]

Yet, Ibsen's play resolves the discussion of sublimation in this essay but also in the previous discussions of Hamsun's early novels. In all these instances, the men attribute supernatural powers onto the women, and only in the case of Iselin and Lyktemann's daughter are these female characters set aside from the main female characters in the story, who possess strong yet typical mortal traits. When contrasting *Når Vi Døde Vågner* with the other stories and excerpts of the novels, one perceives that only Irene is given the task of being both the subject of the mortal and divine. In *Korset*, Rebekka is the divine muse for Bredo, but upon the novel's conclusion a true love prospect for the narrator. First, Ibsen's play demonstrates some of the disastrous dichotomies that art has on artists.

Through an exploration of sublimation in all these cases, one also perceives a framing of sublimation, as if the process were an artform itself. Since it does involve a creative endeavor through the lessening of the libidinal drive, sublimation entails an artistic pursuit and comments on the artist's process in their pursuit of their goals. Yet, each piece of literature frames this process as if the pursuit, and not the result itself, is an object worthy of examination. In Ibsen's play, the entire confession of sublimation and sacrifice is framed as actors portray it in front of an audience, thus adding three-dimensional aspects to this depiction of sublimation. In the case of Bredo, the narrator who loves Rebekka witnesses his admiration for her as the statue possesses her soul. Furthermore, in the case of Hamsun's narrator, the admirer of the Swedish Queen of Sheba, he perceives Kronberg's inspiration from the myth and records it in an article. In this particular case, the narrator further amplifies sublimation by referencing his own article and then, falling for the

Swedish woman who resembles Kronberg's representation of the Queen. In this case, Hamsun is unique in that his representation of sublimation entails an ideal created through the enjoyment of art, rather than using art as a way to satiate feelings for a woman. For this reason, his portrayal stands alone as it privileges the artistic ideal that overpowers the human.

Nonetheless, the three examples show how art imbues the artistic object—painting or stature or story-telling, as seen in the previous two chapters—with a feeling of affection, as if the object could possess traits that might satisfy the artist. Even though it does not completely satisfy all three men, they each experience a momentary pause where the art object did capture their emotions and suspended their human expectations. Only when they remember their human connection to women and the cost of sacrifice for artistry, the men become mournful of the loss of the human manifestation of their ideal. Despite the ideal being just abstract, it briefly captures them when the human briefly embodies this ideal. Thus, the framing of sublimation involves a snapshot of this brief eclipse between the human figure and the ideal—the ideal being more prominent in Hamsun's portrayal.

While the points that female objectification and the incompatibility of art and romance are true, these confrontations with the artistic ideal and reality direct readers to the power of the unspoken, the issues that only art brings out to the open. Since the object of artistic acts and creative acts involve women, these women elicit a form of power that supersedes their objectification. As I discussed earlier in the case of Iselin and Lyktemann's daughter that these women symbolize life, lust, and productivity, the female in these discussions convey power through their ability to uncover the hidden emotions and timeless regenerative quality. These men initially portray the power of their gaze as it is their gaze that fixates on the different women, mortal or supernatural. Yet, as the discussion of sublimation shows, these same men experience the gaze of the woman upon them, and it is this gaze that uncovers not only the unknown desires of men, as I have previously discussed but also transforms the power struggle between men and women. While the men previously assert the power in gazing at the women, the women's gaze on the men shift their own power and transform into objects who retort back to the subject.

Illustration: Camille

Illustration : Woman in Cloth

Chapter 6

A Walk Among the Roses

> [Julius] Kronberg's painting produces a sense of instability both because its subject matter is incomplete and because the Sheban queen's gaze (as well as that of nearly all the other figures) transgresses the beholder.
>
> Elisabeth Oxfeldt, 2003

On a cold Wednesday in February, I go to the Huntington Library, Art Museum, and Botanical Gardens to take pictures of *L'Amour Captif de la Jeunesse*, a statue created after Simon-Louis Boizot and located under a gazebo-like structure. Inspired by Ibsen, Obstfelder, and Hamsun, I consider the idea that art might mediate amorous feelings that a person might feel. I am experimenting with the idea that a particular sculpture might serve as a model for the analyses of sublimation from the aforementioned works. I ask myself, could a rendering of a figure inspired by love possess traits that could illustrate my essay on the subject?

Set in the Rose Garden, I walk amongst the different roses and duck when bees fly by me. I approach the female figure and take pictures, but I get a strange feeling that this figure seems too rapt in mischievous love. *L'Amour Captif de la Jeunesse* seems like an apt name, but the feeling behind the statue clashes with the intention that I wish to create in an illustration. The female figure smiles while her shawl exposes her breast and unaware of the cherub's presence. A little cherub, possibly the manifestation of love, kneels to the side of her and extends a finger to its lips as if prompting us to not tell the youthful woman of its presence. In doing so, cherub as the symbol of love invites the viewer to be part of the event. Tall columns surround both of these figures, and this famous statue is in the middle of the Shakespearean Rose Garden. The cherub, as love, does not seem to be captive of the young woman; rather, the woman appears passive in her unsuspecting smile to the viewer. The cherub's knowing look to the audience mimics the role that actors take when they perform in a play, as they are aware of the audience though the audience members are not part of the play.

After considering how Ibsen's *Når Vi Døde Vågner* displays the troubling aspects of sacrificing life for art, I realize how the different depictions of sublimation might reflect trends of the late nineteenth century. As Per Buvik mentions in his assessment of Irene and Rubek in his article "Kunsten, Kjønnet, og Kvinnen," he indicates how his depiction of Irene shows the literary theme of showing women as having a sexual nature with a deadly destructive tendency. Furthermore, he mentions how writers base their archetypes of such women on biblical women,[197] as Hamsun does in his short-story "Dronningen av Seba." In his article "Irene: Objekt eller Subjekt?" another Ibsen scholar, Frode Helland, compares Irene to Medusa, whose destructive stare gives death to men, as Irene brings Rubek to follow her up the mountain to die in the avalanche.[198] Calling her the gentle version of Medusa, Buvik's view concurs with Helland's assessment that the story, much like other stories of sexualized women during the late nineteenth century, falls into the theme of a woman's destructive sexuality.

This view allows Buvik to assess that Ibsen portrays the fight between the genders for a grasp of power through art and sexuality. Art captures a way to frame societal dangers even in the gaze of love—its destructive gaze, at least in the nineteenth century women, perceives men as they are and stops them in their paths. The stories using art show the folly of men who get caught in the lure of this gaze, yet it freezes the strength of women in one image as if a camera could capture an abstract trait, such as the reversal of power in a connection between men and women.

Meandering through the far western end of the rose gardens, I find the path to the Scholar's Garden blocked. This predicament does not worry me, since most of the statues that I consider drawing are back past the entrance of the rose gardens. I have no other recourse but to retrace my steps back to the entrance of the rose garden.

When I turn to the left, a nearly hidden couple of statues face me. The mud is freshly wet, so I head over by the tips of my toes. I nearly slip on a particularly soft patch of mud to get closer to this unnamed couple of statues. In the center of four slender columns, a naked woman sits blindfolded as a small cherub stands on tiptoes to hold the scarf that shields the woman's eyes. The woman holds the cherub's head of curls with one hand while extended her other hand. The outstretched fingers from this hand reveal the woman's surprised reaction from the insights she is provided by removing her sight. Low relief ornate flowers and plants decorate the base of the columns, and the middle of the slender columns shows plentiful vines with grapes and birds partaking in its juiciness. Since this sculpture mirrors the one in the gardens, I realize that a viewer could see this unnamed sculpture as a preview of the predicament of the young woman who becomes captive of love. If the viewer exits the rose gardens from the direction that I entered into it, the sculpture could also function as the narrative piece showing the consequence of being captive by love. If so, being in love requires a certain amount of blindness.

Just to clarify, the different concepts of Medusa contribute to the way that writers use this figure to suggest a strong woman with a lure that destroys men. The Freudian myth of the Medusa figure symbolizes castration, as her head represents the mother's genitals, thus bringing the threat to men. Freud suggests that the sight of Medusa brings desire while also paradoxically frightening the male, since he is turned into stone and erect.[199] In contrast to the negative association of Medusa, Susan R. Bowers describes the pre-Olympian Gorgon as having origins from North Africa and embodying motherhood with her snakes symbolizing "wisdom and power, healing, immortality, and rebirth."[200] Bowers then mentions how different sources attribute the need to look away from her as a sign of her strong divine power. By citing Nor Hall's *The Moon and the Virgin*, Bowers makes an insightful distinction of "certain woman, death, or gods" as having strong power and compares to "the sun in eclipse."[201] Such a description not only connects strong women to having power to control life and death and having endless time like the sun, but it also captures the different characteristics of strong depictions of women in the nineteenth century.

In contrast to the pre-Olympian Medusa, the Greek story of her origin shows a lack of power and insinuates female rivalry. Bowers explains the story of how Poseidon, god of the sea, rapes beautiful Medusa in Athena's shrine, causing Athena to transform Medusa's lovely hair into a snakes. Later in the story, a brave Perseus uses a shield to protect his gaze from Medusa and reflects her own gaze back at her and beheads her. He then uses her head as a way to counter his enemies by holding it to them to turn them into stone.[202]

According to older literature on psychoanalysis, the Medusa figure symbolizes a rupture in the relationship between women, specifically mothers and daughters. In Arthur A. Miller's psychoanalytic account of a patient's dream of three Gorgons, he asserts how the symbolic meaning of Medusa in dreams reflects his patient's relationship with her mother and her need to have her mother perceive her as an independent woman. Miller further details how his patient's associations of competition with other women and fear of assuming a more traditional woman's role relate to her feelings regarding her mother. Near the end of his assessment, he concludes that the Medusa myth pertains to a tale of competition between Medusa and Athena. The competition between their beauty made Athena turn Medusa into stone.[203]

While such portrayals differ in the treatment of Medusa's power, both accounts underscore her presence as difficult to look at and perceive. In the discussion of literature, these portrayals of Medusa's influence and power reflect the treatment of the mythical and mysterious female figure in late nineteenth century Norwegian literature. Some of the writers explore this power and depict it in supernatural women, while others directly reference Medusa as a distinctly decadent female—the sexually charged and all-perceiving female who possesses some supernatural powers. The women show their power through their gaze, sometimes depicted as a powerful look that perceives men's folly and underlying motives. Other times, this gaze hides its power by camouflaging as a lustful look, a form of communication between two people. The look itself captivates and forms its own lure, a trap that entices both the perceiver and perceived in a game that escapes their conscious awareness. Part of the mysticism in conducting such research is to fall into this lure, but still be able to retain an objective stance at times.

Standing before the nameless statues, I wonder if the sentiment behind this scene and the *L'Amour Captif de la Jeunesse* fit the female figure I wish to draw. Based on my analysis of Irene and Rebekka, I do not find these statues appropriate in sentiment. While the stories conveyed blindness in love, the statue evinces a lighthearted feeling to this predicament. In the woman's embrace of the cherub who blinds her, she seeks to blind herself, an act that the women in the works I analyze do not do. In fact, the men's blindness is exposed to the reader, while the women in the works have that penetrating gaze. In *L'Amour Captif de la Jeunesse*, the statue depicts an unsuspecting woman's fall into love, yet the women I analyze reveal the complexities in falling in love. A reader gets little information about them before they fall in love. In Irene's case, love changes her, while the reader only catches glimpses of Rebekka and less about the Swedish woman who becomes the object of the projected feelings of the Sheban queen. Despite the lack of knowledge about the latter cases, however, the women possess power to unsettle the men, making them overly innocent and blind to the effects of love. These statues, while lovely allegorical works of art, counter this power that knowledge of love's complexities bring, a quality of beauty evident in the female characters.

I keep thinking about the role of Medusa. Why does she keep lurking in these depictions? The relevance of her gaze as that which freezes and enraptures men in return stops me from further making striking points about the text. I am not saying anything new; rather, I retrace the steps others have taken. They stopped in their tracks, so I must examine why they did so and continue because they unearth an underlying assumption that is so clear that we refuse to voice it. Yet, in remaining quiet about it, we have lost the appeal of studying literature for its sake. Instead, we look on to newer conjectures, mechanical structures to adapt a field filled with nuance, and try to compete with the sciences by politicizing our task and mission for studying literary themes. By doing so, we lose the ability to enjoy our literary investigations because a journey into a particular aesthetic theme cannot be intellectualized unless weaponized into a language that aims to destroy the theme in the first place.

While analyzing Ibsen's work in particular, I discovered Beret Wicklund's discussion of Irene and Rubek's relationship as scopophilic, a term that indicates that the relationship is based on the gaze. Since this term describes other interactions between characters I discuss, I start evaluating the different connections between the male and female characters. It is the gaze that gestures a sign of admiration, lust, a romantic connection to the point where the authors feel a strong connection, a shift in their mood at the least.

Wicklund explains how the gaze and its ensuing feelings elicited from the people looking at each other take the place of the physical relationship. She gathers that a scopophilic relationship allows "det seksuelle begjær å komme til uttrykk samtidig som den kroppslige siden ven seksueliteten fornektes."[204] [sexual desire to be expressed while denying the bodily side of sexuality] Like sublimation, sexual expression occurs but not in the way that allows for a typical expression of a romantic or lustful relationship. Yet, here it is, a sign that such a look can function as a form of consummation. How does one define a gaze? Must it involve a mutual prolonged glance between two people?

I walk toward the open field where hedges border its perimeters. I come across Agostino Testa's *The Allegory of Flattery*, a young female figure who plays the flute while a lamb arches its head upward in adoration. Waves of hair crown her head, as all the hair is gathered at the base of the neck before extending down her back. She wears a short-sleeved blouse and a skirt that ties around the back. The lamb's head pushes the skirt upward and exposes her legs. The woman stands playing a flute, as if her music talents flatter someone. Although the placard nearby mentions some details, it does not mention whether the lamb flatters the woman or the woman partakes in playing to flatter someone. The figure stands in front of a large camellia bush, and one of the browned and aged camellias rests on the bend of her elbow. Since the placard mentions not to touch the statue, I do not remove this flower but wonder if this particular addition from nature adds to my fascination with it. The young woman diverts her gaze downward and away from the viewer, as if feeling an emotion through her playing. Viewers might consider how their presence contributes her pull away from them. In contrast to the other statues where one woman looked past the viewer while another gladly accepted to cover her sight, this particular figure portrays the way that an art practice makes the artist derive energy from inward, at least while partaking in it. Parts of the statue are darkened from the sculptor's method of chipping away at the limestone. Unlike the smooth marbled surface of the other statues, this figure shows deeper crevices in her face, arms and clothing. The effect is that the woman appears to age despite looking young, even though everyone knows that statues cannot age, at least not in the human sense.

When checking the Oxford Dictionary, I find several entries of the word as a verb, noun, and even in literary theory:

> Verb: look steadily and intently, especially in admiration, surprise, or thought.
>
> Noun: a steady intent look.

In literary theory: a particular perspective taken to embody certain aspects of the relationship between observer and observed, especially as reflected in the way in which an author or film direction unconsciously or otherwise directs attention.

An interesting note – *gaze* is derived from the late Middle English term gaw or gawk.

The definition of the word implies a relationship between an observed and observer, yet it does not necessarily indicate the type of connection, if there is any. When I consider the definition of *gawk*, I find it to mean to stare or gaze stupidly, attributing the action with an amount of ridicule, as if the looker is caught in surprise to the extent that they no longer possess an intelligent thought. Yet, a gawk is a particular kind of gaze, so the latter term need not involve the former's connotation. The word gaze has an ambiguity, as it does not put restrictions on the observed or observer, only that the observer watches the observed without necessarily needing reciprocation from them.

Since this relationship does not limit an observer to a specific time nor the observed to a particular setting, I wonder about extending a gaze to an examination of the literature I study. The men in these stories gaze at certain women, some whose intense stare beckons them to return the gesture. More importantly, I see their gaze as their psychological framework that affects their fascination with these women no matter how slight their connection. My investigation peers into the actions of these men, who are unaware of my actions. As I draw certain symbols after making my initial analysis about their work, I authenticate my gaze back at the stories in order to recreate them and infuse them with the energy I perceive the stories have. In doing so, I am enacting the gaze of a woman witnessing the male gaze onto female characters who captivate them with their prolonged hard look. While this does make me wonder whether I am a voyeur of sorts, I do know that I wish to understand whether their gaze necessitates the bad reputation that the male gaze entails.

The wind blows and competes with the sun's attempt to warm me. I take some pictures and quickly draw the contour. In my earlier years in art school, I used to proceed quickly to the details of the figure in live model drawing sessions. Time has not changed this tendency. By shading the dark eroded parts, my notice of the statue's unintended flaws shows up in the drawing, even though that feature impedes on the statue's beauty. Yet, the darkened areas juxtaposed to the highlights on the statue's figure show starkness and a drastic quality to the statue. Hearing more voices behind me, I quickly put the drawing back into my temporary portfolio case—a makeshift folder made from cardboard—and take out my camera to capture the figure. I step away to allow the others to enjoy the view of the statue, and they do so quickly before moving onto the next one. After I collect my belongings, I walk toward the exit of the gardens.

Considering the layers of this experiment, I wonder if my gaze seeks to penetrate the literary works and further enhance my understanding of the works by drawing an art piece while reflecting on my analysis. By looking at all the intertextual signifiers of the text, artwork, my analysis, and my rendering, I think about my gaze in a psychoanalytic content. Hal Foster connects the Medusa's petrifying gaze to Lacan's discussion of the painting as a metaphor for his description of the screen in the gaze. Throughout Foster's explication of Lacan's ideas, he aptly describes the dual screen that shields us from the gaze from this alterior other, yet also allows us to tame it. Forster explains further "painting might aim to arrest the gaze before the gaze can arrest us, as if the very gestures of such a composition might preempt the violence of the gaze"[205] thus implying that the screen might allow the subject to do the same. The screen protects us from the notion that the Real does not follow our logic and construct—as Foster indicates as "a black hole, a negative space of non-sociality…of non-subjectivity"[206] so it would annihilate us by default.

When speaking about the gaze in relation to subjectivity, Lacan discusses the scopic field and how one's vision, and in particular, one's eyes, limit one's perception of self. He defines the gaze as "In our relation to things, in so far as this relation is constituted by the way of vision, and ordered in the figures of representation, something slips, passes, is transmitted, from stage to stage, and is always to some degree eluded in it—that is what we call the gaze."[207] Lacan's discussion refers to the subject's split between the self who experiences and a view of herself outside of himself. This view is always kept apart from the experiencing subject, as the subject cannot perceive himself outside of his own perspective. It is this exterior perspective, one that is outside of an experiencing subject, that the subject attempts to adapt himself to, but also vanishes because he is apart from it. In regard to desire, the subject may regard herself in those he desires, but it also reduces her to a level of incomprehension. The gaze reduces the subject to a sense of self outside of the self, thus showing an annihilation of self-mastery.

Considering the difficulty in giving a concrete example of this predicament, I wonder if this abstract theoretical discussion of the Lacanian gaze prohibits any scholar from making the correlation between our criticism of older literature and the subject and the gaze from the Real. Yet, this gaze is not the gaze that I am discussing for I am still working within a human subjectivity that does not annihilate the works. If I am indeed using my gaze to annihilate the works of these Norwegian writers, I use it to recreate symbols through writing conventions and then illustrating an image to fully portray the symbol. Despite it being an annihilation, I feel like it is an act of love, an awakening, a revival. And if other scholars are more critical and more transgressive in their analyses, does my act of destruction come with a softening touch?

After making myself a cup of tea, I settle at my desk and take out the drawing. Artists always say to draw from one's observations in reality instead of drawing from an image, albeit a digital image whose lighting distorts the reality of the image. I check my phone to see 80 percent battery power and head to my room where I draw *The Allegory of Flattery*. I email the image to my computer where I can look at it, while using my phone to play music. I put water in a small plastic cup and open up my small watercolor paints. After scrolling through and finding a random dark academia playlist, I take out the drawing that I had stared at the gardens before it got too crowded and continue the process. As I draw the figure, I do not render the lamb, as I should consider changing the depiction for this image. Then, I use the white paint to highlight the lights of this drawing.

I darken the parts where rain damaged the statue, hardening her look to better reflect Irene's condition, a beautiful statue-like woman whose disappointments stiffened her physical form. These aspects still attract Rubek and compel him to follow her up a mountain, an act that inevitably leads him to his death, or a reawakening to life. Or does it reflect Rebekka? The sensuous nature in which Bredo, the artist friend of the narrator in Obstfelder's *Korset*, displays in his rendering of Rebekka alludes more to the marbled statues. In fact, Obstfelder does not reveal too much of what the drawings entail, only that they capture her soul. Such obscurities make it easier for the reader to witness the narrator's emotional landscape as opposed to the qualities that Bredo captured from Rebekka. The gaze of the figure in *The Allegory of Flattery* reflects her moved state as she plays the flute. This powerful inward turn that ignores the viewer and any external stimuli refers to an emotion that one experiences when engaged in the craft of art. Though separate from Oxfeldt's sharp analysis of the four levels of intertextual layers in Hamsun's "Dronningen av Seba," this figure alludes to the realization that Hamsun's narrator makes about the painter Kronberg's rendering of the queen's gaze.

Oxfeldt mentions that the narrator initially finds the figure ambiguous in terms of gender and ethnicity, making her appear more European than Oriental and a curious mix of gender attributes. Then, Oxfeldt explains that the Sheban queen's gaze in Kronberg's painting addresses the narrator's feelings about witnessing this painting. She states,

"Subsequently the narrator uses his descriptions of her eyes to convince himself (and his interlocutor/reader) that what he felt upon seeing the painting was something reminiscent of love rather than fear and ambivalence."[208] This insight reminds me that the statue playing the flute displays a type of love for the craft of music. While the statues I previously examined directly reference the interference of love, the figures do not demonstrate a woman's active role in partaking in it. The Sheban queen's gaze, as in the statue of the Allegory, actively assess the value of their surroundings, whether internal or external or for the purpose of clarifying a rumor or offering a response to someone simply to flatter them.

My experiment ends with the selection of this particular drawing as the one to illustrate the ideas from the essay I am writing. Though Medusa's gaze pertains to different connotations of female sexuality and female power, one might refer to it as a penetrating gaze that seeks to understand the complexities of the way the male characters love the women. In the works that I analyze, art functions as the receptacle of seeing one's love reflected for the sake of understanding, at least momentarily so. Yet, none of the male characters understand their love for the women. In the case of Hamsun's narrator, he does not understand the affection he feels for the Swedish woman, but he might better understand his fascination with Kronberg's depiction of the Sheban queen. This experiment is intended to reflect the men's actions back to them not for moral purposes, but more so as a reflection of the gaze.

Unlike the Lacanian Real, I go deeper into symbols to prolong the enjoyment of reading these works and understanding them. The natural progression of ideas does not surprise me when I consider Jan Jagodzinski's discussion of art and the construction of the ego-ideal. He states, "Lacan's discussion of the evil eye that accompanied aphanisis, the fading of the subject and its alienation as a castrating eye (of the Freudian Medusa), always took the form of a sublimation, the need for art to protect (frame) the subject from the full effects of the Real, which could lead to trauma."[209] Yet, unlike Jagodzinski's discussion to find a dimension that avoids the delusion of the Symbolic, I decide to further engage in it. In selecting a statue unrelated to the material I analyze, I see the irony of depicting a woman who plays the flute as a means of communication—

flattery, a seemingly disingenuous appeal to others—as a way to continue the use of art to frame myself from the Lacanian Real. Though I often have to reread Jagodzinski's allusion to sublimation, I finally understand it though in a different context.

For me to better understand the role of sublimation—or rather, my fascination with it—in the works that I analyze, I follow the compulsion to continue the trend of using art to frame my own love for the subjects. This love, however, does not endanger me to the paths that the male characters endure, only has me find my own path along a similar direction, though in different contexts. The intertextual richness in Hamsun's "Dronningen av Seba" shows how the narrator finds some clarity in his feelings In regard to art yet only through further exploration of analysis of the Kronberg's painting, though it obscures his ability to perceive reality and the Swedish woman's lack of feelings for him. Yet, the discussion of the painting in the story shows the possibility for clarity in one's feelings for art. Hamsun's technique for creating multiple textures of stories within the main narrative, as discussed as sublimation in the previous chapters, reveals the structure of love for the characters. Despite being seen as little interruptions from the main narrative, these eccentric micronarratives explain for the troubles of love in the main narrative.

For this reason, the choice of the flute-playing figure as the model is apt in that I use the figure to illustrate key ideas, and that figure also engages in the art practice. Months later, I discover the coincidence of my choice of this sculpture and my decision to end my essay on *Pan* and *Victoria* with Lacan's allusion of the myth of Pan and Syrinx. Whether my intuition or unconscious tampered with my decision, some essence directed me on that day in February.

Illustration: The Allegory of Flattery

Chapter 7

Iselin Revisited: Mystery of Two Identities Resolved

In my earlier days of analyzing Hamsun's work, I was told to examine the lesser-known play, *Munken Vendt*, to resolve the differences between it and my analysis of the characters of one well-known work. This play reveals a haphazard plot structure and chronicles the rebellious actions of a monk who pursues different women and shuns them for spite. After reading this play, I resolve the mystery of how Hamsun used the same names of characters in *Pan* with seemingly different personality traits. My discussion in this essay unravels the mystery I resolved, at least for those thinkers who entertain the idea that the characters are one and the same.

Zupančič's essay "Love as Comedy" immediately draws out Lacan's definition of sublimation as a process that condescends the desired object in order for the subject to experience jouissance. In my original analysis, I had made the distinction of desire and love but did not consider it as clearly as Zupančič. She presents an analysis of the Lacanian notion of love as comical since it supposes a different aim than desire and consists of a different process. She initially poses the question to the reader, "Is love not always the worshipping of a sublime object, even though it doesn't always take as radical a form as in the case of courtly love?"[210] In the process of sublimation, a person makes the person they are in-love with as a powerful sublime object, a work of art as in the case of courtly love. Yet, she explains how love entails a desublimation process, or a process in which a person devalues the sublime aspect of a person. In desire, the person maintains the goal of ennobling the other person.

She defines love as the process of "*preserving the transcendence in the very accessibility of the other.*"[211] Following this logic, one sees how one loves different sides of a person. She states that one accepts the sublime and banal aspects of a person, and also the slight difference between what one knows of a person and what one does not know. This slight difference is what Zupančič refers to as minimal difference or "the Other as different from her-or himself"[212] though her explanation using a Charlie Chaplin movie provides humor to one's understanding. While I did write about this process in previous academic essays, especially in the stories that struck me so vibrantly, I considered the difference between love and desire. If the men in the literary works desire the women, it makes sense that they replicate it with signifiers to maintain their desire. Yet, in Hamsun's *Pan*, he writes that Glahn says that he loves the dream the most. The dream is Iselin, the beautiful forest spirit. It makes me think if Glahn loves her due to his physical experiences of her as a metonym for nature itself, which might be an example of the sublime.

Without having to rearticulate all my analyses on the subject—otherwise I should just reread my own essays—I do consider how the writers write about men who use creativity and artistic means as a way to maintain the desire. I consider how the means of art might also enable love despite the fact that art is a means of beautifying and ennobling one's perspective of an object represented. By using the means of drawing aspects of the objects that the characters sublimated, I seek to understand this exact process by also engaging in the process of drawing images that pertain to the sublime object that the writers portray.

I question whether the object I draw makes this object—what scholars in this trajectory refer to as "Das Ding/The Thing"—concrete or pushes it farther in the inaccessible realm. While the different associations of objects, the signifiers, continue to spread as different readers enjoy the literary works, I stop to consider the drawing that reflects how I think about the Thing of each literary work. In the case of Hamsun, it is Iselin, Iselin as creativity, the Queen of Sheba, and the way art captures a myth. For Obstfelder, it is Rebekka but also the bonds of unspoken love. For Ibsen, it is the idea of Irene as a work of art in "The Resurrection" and Irene herself. As I have shown in my analyses, Ibsen and Obstfelder demonstrate a discrepancy between the woman that the men desire and the statues bearing their likeness. In both examples, the statues capture an essence of the women apart that alludes to the Thing, yet the human version exemplifies the banal object that Zupančič refers to in her discussion of love in sublimation.

Yet, in Hamsun's examples, the creative act either through storytelling and writing about art also generates a way that the drive extends beyond the woman. For this reason, his protagonists fail in capturing the women they love, though I can now see that it may allow them to persist in their desire for the women. After comparing his representation of it with other authors who take on the same theme, I am more aware of how correct I am of my assessment of his work. In his case, he represents love and desire occurring at once towards the same object, yet different aspects of those objects. As Zupančič states in relation to the difference between the aim of desire and love, "In love, we do not find satisfaction in the other we aim at; we find it in the space or gap between, to put it bluntly, what we see and what we get."[213] To clearly situate in Hamsun's work, the male protagonists wish to get satisfaction from the human counterparts of the ideal, yet he desires the ideal generated through nature and creativity. It also does not help that his protagonists use the word "love" to refer to their feelings for desire. This reason also explains for the male protagonists maintain their amorous feelings at various intensities as well as a pulling away of a pursuit despite these feelings. Yet, I question what happens when love and desire are separate. More specifically, I question the identity of Iselin in Hamsun's last depiction of her and attempt to resolve the puzzle of whether she is the same mythological nature spirit. For the past couple of years, her seeming difference gnawed at me until I looked further into the text for the sake of resolving this seeming incongruency between a sensuous nature spirit and a strong, mysterious woman.

Most Hamsun scholars analyze the characters Iselin, Didrik (Diderik in *Pan*), Dundas, and Svend Herlufsen as they appear in different ways in *Pan*, *Victoria*, and *Munken Vendt*. According to Buttry, she describes Iselin from *Munken Vendt* as having no resemblance to Iselin of *Pan*, as she is not the "embodiment of eros,"[214] as even I myself alluded to in an earlier essay. Buttry mentions that Blis from *Munken Vendt* possesses more of the feminine traits that Iselin of *Pan* conveys, as Iselin from *Munken Vendt* shows more coldness and cruelty. Though Buttry's analysis of transgression and desire in Munken Vendt alludes to similarities between the characters from *Pan* and *Mysterier*, Buttry focuses mainly on her analyses of Munken, the titular character, and his mission to show the strength of human will.

Similar to the views of scholar Even Arntzen, I agree that these characters are mythological in *Pan* and *Victoria*, but they take on a more realistic portrayal in *Munken Vendt*. As Arntzen states in his assessment of Iselin in *Pan*, main character Lieutenant Glahn mixes reality and myth until he cannot tell the difference between the two, so this fact supports the view that when he perceives Iselin, he cannot tell if she is appearing in reality or just in his mind.[215] For this reason, the entire play *Munken Vendt* takes on a realistic depiction of a mythological story.

I take the oppositional view that these characters from *Pan* and *Victoria* are the same characters in *Munken Vendt*. The difference between depictions between Iselin in *Pan* and Iselin in *Munken Vendt* becomes clearer when one takes the view that the play positions the characters as mortal characters who then become mythologized in *Pan* and *Victoria*. By examining certain similarities to Iselin of *Pan* and examining her role as one who elicits creative energy, as seen in her interaction with Svend Herlufsen, I show the possibility of how the characters are the same. In seeing Iselin as the same as the mythological counterpart, I reveal how the realistic counterpart shows the residue from the dreamlike portrayal. The dream fixes the disappointments presented from the realistic counterpart.

This eight-act play differs from the content in *Pan* and *Victora*, thus it focuses more on Munken Vendt's decision to transgress social norms and then repent for them. Since the play comments on the importance of human will as opposed to a belief in God, the characters demonstrate a change in fate, such as the loss of a home or conversion into Christianity, which are important topics for discussions on human will as the determining agent in bringing about a particular fate. For the context of this discussion, however, I do focus primarily on Iselin and her ability to elicit creative energy in order to posit that the reality of a dream often shows displacement of certain aspects and an origin of regret.

Similarities between *Pan*'s Iselin and Iselin of *Munken Vendt*

While I do not deny that Iselin in *Munken Vendt* is colder and more severe than her counterpart in *Pan* and *Victoria,* I find clues to suggest she is the same character. In *Pan*, Lieutenant Glahn mentions that Iselin has Didrik, Dundas, and Svend Herlufsen as her lovers, and Glahn as the main protagonist claims to love her. While another character, Blis, does act as sensuous as Iselin does in *Pan*, Iselin of *Munken Vendt* elicits attention and desire from these men, though she refuses them due to upholding the norms of a noblewoman. In the early scene in Iselin's house, Didrik hints that he wishes to propose to her, to which Iselin simply tells him to put his hat on his head—a phrase she repeats throughout the play to show her frustration with him.

Even when Munken Vendt first sees her, he stares at her for a long time and invites her to his camp in a nearby mountain. Dundas and Svend joke with each other that Iselin does not give them hope that she returns their affections. Even at the end when years have passed, Esben Skomager still addresses her and mistakenly refers to her when Munken Vendt admires a pretty young woman. During this brief exchange, a group of young women in addition to Didrik driving a carriage with Iselin inside, Munken Vendt makes an observation on the lovely young women but does not specify whom he refers. Esben makes a mistake and comments that Iselin will never find an equal to her beauty. While they these male characters only function as admirers in the play, this aspect heightens in the dreamlike setting in *Pan* and *Victoria.* Within a dreamlike setting, this quality to Iselin gives them the attribute of being lovers even if they were never so in *Munken Vendt.*

Pan's Iselin is known for her gaze and her ability to be in her garden during the midnight sun. She embodies the abundance of nature. Though these are minor details, they offer evidence of Iselin's character that coincides with her from earlier depictions. When Iselin of Os meets Munken Vendt at the beginning of the story, she notes his fiery gaze at Blis. She remarks on it and states, "Hun tækkes Jær, Pigen der"[216] [She likes you, the girl there] and "Hvorhelst I end vender Jærs Øje saa træffer det hende og træffer nøje"[217] [Wherever you turn your eye, it hits her and hits it closely]. Referring to his gaze in a poetic way, Iselin notes to Munken how much he conveys through his penetrating gaze, a trait that her counterpart in *Pan* also becomes associated with. When she addresses him and invites him to seek shelter on her farm, she presents the same forwardness that she does in *Pan*. She states to him:

> I længes fasted til den Pige som gik? Se se hvor det traf. I fik Ild I Jærs Blik. Fortæl mig hvad meget I lærte paa Skole. Stor blev I derude og snar som en Fole…Det falder mig ind, I har Hjem i et Fjæld, til Vinteren kommer den lange Kvæld,--jeg byr Jær en Stue som ingen bor i. Den kunde I ha for Jær selv. Hvad tror I?[218]

> [Are you longing to go to the girl who left? Look where it hit. You caught fire in your gaze. Tell me how much you learned at school. You got big out there and fast as a foal…It occurs to me you have a home in a mountain, until the winter comes the long night, I offer you a room in which no one lives. You could have that for yourself. What do you think?]

Despite not propositioning herself to be his lover, Iselin does invite him to stay with her and beckons him to consider her thought by asking him for his opinion. Though not overtly sexual, she does break the norm of a passive woman who merely accepts a man's proposal. In addition to rejecting the proposals of Dundas, Svend, and Didrik, she reverses Munken's invitation to go with him to his mountain and accepts him on her terms. Similar to *Pan*'s Iselin as a nature spirit who invites Glahn into her part of the forest, Iselin proposes for Munken to stay with her and tell her his stories of his studies. She even mentions that he has longing for Blis, which might initially dispel another woman's affections, but it continues to push Iselin further into her convictions to invite him. Due to the stark differences in *Pan*'s Iselin's softness and Iselin's temperamental attitude, scholars and readers alike perceive them as completely different. Yet, the clues of their similarities provide an origin story for Iselin.

In *Pan*, Iselin addresses her first time of intimacy with Dundas and mentions being in her garden in the morning and not awakening her maid. This softness in tone does show remarkable similarities to Blis. After all, Blis marries Dundas and has an affair with Didrik, so readers might easily attribute her character with Iselin of *Pan.* Yet, in her early conversation with Dundas, Iselin gives him the ambiguous answer of "Nej, Ung Dundas, I ved vi er kvit"[219] [No, young Dundas, you know we are done.] when Svend reminds Dundas that she turned him down years ago. The vagueness in the response of acknowledging that they are done might infer that they did have a relationship earlier or some understanding of a connection which has passed. Given that most people refer to Iselin as a virgin maiden, readers assume that Iselin only refers to being done with Dundas' request to go out with her. In the scene in *Pan* when Iselin talks to Glahn about her first moment of intimacy with Dundas, she mentions her garden outside her chambers. In one of the later scenes in the play, Iselin mentions to Didrik that she stays in her garden while Didrik stays inside. In one of her last scenes with Munken, she mentions to him that she stays outside: "Ja Natten var stille. Jeg soled mig længe. Og Solen laa varm over alle Enge. Men dèr laa den rød"[220] [Yes, the night was quiet. I sunbathed for a long time. And the sun lay watch over all the meadows. But there it lay red]. This small detail refers to her willingness to spend time outside during the nighttime much like her counterpart in *Pan.*

Even though Hamsun does not suggest that Iselin experiences intimacy with any of her male admirers, he does allude to a repressed sexual nature that only comes out through his observations of her and through her interactions with Svend. At the end when Iselin and Munken share a revelation of his motives concerning his return to her property in Os, Iselin refers to him as a wolf and surmises correctly that he will fight endlessly and relentlessly. In this interaction, however, she admits a part of her behavior in the past that no one witnesses, so readers can only believe her. She states, "Selv er jeg saa ond og uendelig syndig, i Aar har jeg vildret paa dette Sted; men Trodsen slap op, jeg slog Øjnene ned…Paa det blev jeg kyndig…"[221] [I myself am so wicked and infinitely sinful, this year I have been wrong in this place; but the defiance gave way, I lowered my eyes…I became knowledgeable about that]. Since she does wish to connect with Munken, she does admit to certain foolish forms of behavior that no one admits due to her position in the town. Hamsun certainly does not write them in the play, yet one might consider her previous action of releasing Munken when he was initially judged to be jailed. Iselin's confession presents her own critical nature as she judges herself to be sinful and acknowledges the experience of having to endure the guilt that her sins brought. Since no one in the town perceives these sins, readers wonder at the nature of these transgressions.

One example of her sin might be her attempt to emotionally connect with Munken. When Munken tells her to meet her the next day, it disrupts her usual day to day expectations. Didrik asks her about her changed attitude and his words address the changed behavior as he himself states that her words are "den stærkeste siden vor hele Forening"[222] [the strongest since our entire union]. In regard to her behavior, he states, "Din Færd, dine ændrede Skikke, din søvnløse Nat, dine slørede Blikke. Jeg spurgte dig mygt om den Kvide du bar. Du løj: det var Vaaren, den kommende Hede."[223] [Your movements, your changed customs, your sleepless night, your blurred looks. I asked you softly about the anguish you carried. You lied: It was spring, the coming heat.] Though the characters do not say more about her behavior, Iselin does show a difference from her usual attitude toward Didrik. Readers surmise that this change alludes to Munken's return. Throughout the whole play, Iselin shows interest in Munken, who claims to not love her.

As Buttry mentions, Munken declares to love Blis, then Alexa as a symbol of Blis' innocence, yet chooses to visit Iselin and not pursue Blis. This discrepancy between his proclaimed love and hidden desire marks the difference in love and desire as better explained in Zupančič's discussion of the Lacanian Real. She states the following:

> The whole point of the Lacanian concept of the Real is that the impossible happens…It is not something that happens when we want it, or try to make it happen, or expect it, or are ready for it. It always happens at the wrong time and in the wrong place; it is always something that doesn't fit the (established or the anticipated) picture. The Real as impossible means that there is no right time or place for it, and not that it is impossible for it to happen.[224]

Yet also, Zupančič mentions a similar disorienting experience when considering the difference between desire and love as an experience that happens outside of its time and context. By framing her analysis of the concept as similar to the time warp in science fiction novels, she explains:

> This time warp essentially refers to the fact that a piece of some other (temporal) reality get caught in our present temporality (or vice versa), appearing there where there is no structural place for it, thus producing a strange, illogical tableau. Something appears where it should not be and thus breaks or interrupts the linearity of time, the harmony of the picture.[225]

In both assessments, Zupančič refers to love occurring without expectation since it arrives without the intention of either person. In the context of romantic love, it exists as a factor that disrupts the norm. In both assessments of two different processes, I find the correlation between time and linearity worth noting. Of the Real, she notes that "it happens at the wrong time and wrong place"[226] and "breaks or interrupts the linearity of time."[227] Another similarity involves the example of the picture. Zupančič first notes that the Real "doesn't fit the established or anticipated picture"[228] and that the disruption of something appearing where it should not result in a "strange, illogical tableau" and breaks "the harmony of the picture."[229] In terms of her explanations of the concepts, she aptly alludes to the harrowing aspect of the Real and proves her point as to why love is comical in an ironic sense.

This explanation offers this discussion a few benefits. It helps to resolve the difference between the Iselins, as it explains how Munken Vendt separates love and desire in a way that Glahn could not. Zupančič's explanation of love in the Lacanian Real helps readers to understand Munken's strange actions toward both Blis and Iselin; he claims to love one while seeking to talk to the other, a claim that Buttry states when she assesses Munken's transgressions and inconsistency in behavior. His last act of being tied to a tree with soil in his hands could demonstrate his devotion to her, or as Buttry claims a lack of internal security. Furthermore, Joseph Wiehr asserts that Iselin loves Munken Vendt and remains passionately in love with him for years, resulting in her death when she realizes that he becomes seriously injured.[230] Yet, one of the more overlooked signs of love is that of Svend Herlufsen's humorous monologues on his unwavering admiration for Iselin. This view counters Wiehr's perspective of Svend's character as "the cynic, who proclaims views of women savoring very strongly of Also sprach Zarathustra..."[231] While I do not dismiss this characterization of Svend, as he does use his poetic monologues to vent his frustration, my unorthodox reading of his character only makes sense when taking on the view of love in the Real as a shift from the conventional readings of this play.

Zupančič states of love occurring at the wrong time and place and forming a strange tableau, and such descriptors refer to the comical frustration that Svend feels as he proclaims his love for Iselin and her subtle yet cunning gestures towards him. In the main interpretation of the play, readers see how Iselin only loves Munken yet marries Didrik. Nonetheless, she treats both coldly. Though her actions have ulterior motives, she persists in showing kindness to Svend while flirting with him. Her playful and joyful behavior around Svend Herlufsen proves that her effect on him evinces her transgression behind closed doors. It alludes to the sins she confesses to Munken and exemplifies some of the transformation of the mind that Didrik mentions to which she declares that such transformation is more than she understands.

Despite receiving long monologues from Munken, Iselin does inspire poetic imagery from Svend, whose admiration for Iselin continues into their middle-aged years. A minor side character whose poetic diatribes elicit humor and amusement from the reader, Svend contrasts with Dundas whose easy-going disposition allows him to dispel of love's refusals. In *Pan*, Hamsun mentions Svend as one of Iselin's lovers but does not offer any other descriptions of him. In my previous analyses when I comment on how Iselin inspires creative energy, she still inspires this energy but mainly from Svend Herlufsen in *Munken Vendt*.

Throughout the play, she shows favoritism toward him. At the beginning when Didrik, Dundas and Svend enter her place, Iselin ensures that he receive a favorable seat as she expresses, "Svend Herlufsens Sæde Skal være just dèr, paa det blødeste Klæde"[232] [Svend Herlufsen's seat must be right there, on the softest cloth.] Later in the play when Svend needs to demand payment from Didrik in court, Iselin coyly persuades him not to do so. Though she has ulterior motives to not lose money through her husband's increasing debts, her gestures toward Svend display tenderness that she does not even show to her husband. In this exchange between Iselin and Svend, readers see her open display of affection:

> Iselin: Da kender jeg daarligt min skattede Ridder. I kaldte mig engang Jærs Hjærtes Besidder--?
>
> Svend Herlufsen: Det er I…Jeg mener, vig bort fra min Vej….
>
> Iselin: (lægger Haanden paa hans Arm) I vil ikke fordre den Bøde?
>
> Svend Herlufsen: (forvirret) Jo….Nej.[233]
>
> [Iselin: Then I hardly know my treasured Knight. You once called me the possessor of your heart?
>
> Svend Herlufsen: It's you.... I mean, get out of my way...
>
> Iselin: (puts her hand on his arm) You won't demand that fine?
>
> Svend Herlufsen: (confused) Yeah...No.]

Though readers never see the scene where Svend calls her the possessor of his heart, his response to her confirms it. After years pass, Didrik's debt become so large that he loses Iselin's farm, prompting Svend to make a payment so that she can get it back. In a court scene, Iselin demands attention by speaking in a loud and clear voice to express Svend's intentions. She states,

> Svend Herlufsen staar her. Vor kæreste Ven vil sikkert bestaa os sin Yndest igen. Vil Didrik, min Mand, købe Gaarden tilbage er Svend den Vorherre som alting kan mage. Hans Ord bør vel høres til sidste Slut.[234]
>
> [Svend Herlufsen is standing here. Our dearest friend will surely bestow his favor on us again. If Didrik, my husband, wants to buy the farm back, Svend is the Master who can do anything. His words should be heard to the end].

With words that show more praise to Svend than she does to her husband, Iselin masks her admiration for him through her motives to save her livelihood. Certainly she wishes to have the life she is accustomed to, but her words show her esteem for Svend. By referring to him as a dearest friend and the Lord who can do anything, Iselin makes her regard for Svend public, though he wishes to see it through intimacy. Given the contrast of her extreme caustic behavior toward Didrik and Munken, this softness she shows to Svend reflects a different side to her, one that likely surpasses her own understanding of herself. Even until the very end, she sees Svend and calls him a faithful friend, a term that might be open to interpretation. For instance, she does label him a friend as opposed to a lover, yet her actions show her love for him that develops by accident and without her awareness of it.

As Zupančič explains, love in the Real comes at the wrong time and the wrong place, thus making it possible that the manifestation of love in this play develops between two unlikely characters. Since the union between Svend and Iselin is not the focus of this play, readers consider their interactions impertinent to the main plot and theme of the story. Yet, their interactions point to the accidental love relationship between them, the interaction that happens outside of the usual discussion for this play. Since Iselin's question to Svend concerning his allusion to her as a possessor of his heart occurred outside of the reader's witness of the play, this particular exchange exemplifies how their love falls outside of their expectations. Readers can attest that she marries Didrik out of convenience and might desire a certain kind of affection from Munken, yet she mistreats them in different ways. Through her actions, readers perceive her disfavor for them, but she reserves kindness for Svend. Since Iselin and Svend do not consummate their affections, Svend continues to desire her as she never stops being the sublime person.

Similar to my discussion of Iselin as a creative force in *Pan* and *Victoria*, Iselin from *Munken Vendt* inspires Svend to develop his poetic monologues that describe his feelings for her but also portray his perspective of the events at hand. Though they often elicit amusement for Dundas, they do provide a way to counter the main narrative. At the beginning of the play when Dundas, Didrik, and Svend flirt with Iselin, Dundas asks Svend about his feelings about his love, and Svend responds with the following:

Der lever i Ostindien en Rov-Edderkop af Skabning og af Farve som en rød Orchidé. Den ligger midt i Dagen forat ses og at se, med Ben til alle Kanter og med Bugen vendt op. Den ligger der saa længe og urørlig som Døden.

Og Sommerfuglen kender ej den Rov-Edderkop, han svirrer om den herlige, den røde Orchidé som ligger midt i Dagen og hver Sommerfugl kan se.

Han flyver ned paa Blomsten. Han flyver aldrig op. Han fløj i Favn med Døden.

Saa ligger Orchidéen der saa livløs som før. Men nye Sommerfuglegyrer søger den—og dør. Og hver Gang ligger Blomsten der urørlig igen.

Min Kærest er som den.[235]

[There lives in the East Indies a predatory spider of the form and Color of a red Orchid. It lies in the middle of the day to be seen and to see, with legs to all sides and with the belly turned up. It lies there as long and immovable as Death.

And the Butterfly doesn't know the Predatory Spider, he flutters about the glorious, red Orchid that lies in the middle of the day and every Butterfly can see. He flies down on the flower. He never flies up. He flew in the arms of Death.

Then the Orchid lies there as lifeless as before. But new Butterfly ants seek it—and die. And each time the flower lies there immovable again.

My love is like that].

By constructing a powerful imagery of the spider that appears as a luring red orchid that captures its prey, Svend portrays his feelings about desiring—though he uses the word love—a woman whose response to him kills him. Dundas responds with a jest that his description of his love is so accurate that she is as red as Iselin's beret, yet in this comment Dundas addresses the accuracy of Svend's metaphor. This metaphor of Iselin as a spider who looks like a red orchid depicts her as someone lovely but preys upon the admiration of others. By comparing himself to a butterfly, Svend brings the imagery of himself as a joyful person who only seeks a beautiful woman but understands too late of her danger. Yet, Svend also demonstrates that love involves a concealment of one's nature that leads to death. Svend's description of butterflies as men also illustrates their particular vulnerability. While I do consider his feelings for her as desire, as he never become knowledgeable of her as her husband does, he does see her strictness as predatory as it lures him. When addressing Iselin, he states, "Men pine mig gør I iblandt tildøde, da taler min Galskab, jeg slipper et Pist"[236] [But if you torment me among the death, my madness speaks, and I release a sting]. His unwavering closeness to her throughout the play makes a reader interpret his feelings toward her as love, as he sees her worst behavior and still puts himself through the misery of being denied. Yet, Zupančič describes, love in the Real never happens when people are ready for it. Even though Svend is aware of it, Iselin might push these feelings away.

During another scene when Svend asks for a sum of five thousand speciedaler, which was the Norwegian currency before the kroner, in court and asks for it before the magistrate, Iselin's flirtatious behavior makes him rescind his demand, yet he still offers a poetic monologue in the middle of court. Since he takes back his charge for the payment five thousand dollars due to Iselin's request, readers perceive that he still admires her. While not as coherent as the first monologue, Svend does admit to feelings of love but also a woman's vulnerability. No one responds to counter the validity of his words, as they are treated as merely nonsensical words for the amusement of the court. Yet, Iselin does allude to his professed claim that Svend had told her she was the possessor of his heart. He admits his feelings after his allusion to his enflamed heart,

> Jeg steg mig ind i Stuen, kun Maanen stod og saa derpaa…og der var blot et Mundens Nej hos Duen, hun krummed sig og krammed sig saa fro. Vi brused blinde sammen begge to. Saa døde Ild og Gløder ud paa Gruen. Mit Hjærte det laa rødt og grovt og lo.

Og vældigt havde Kærligheden hende, hun var mig helt

> hjærtinderlig min Brud. Men denne Gang tog al min Fryd en Ende: Jeg nejer mig i Grus paa hendes Bud, jeg ber til henne som jeg ber til Gud—forgæves alt…Fy Fanden, for Elende, en Pibebrand som aldrig slukkes ud![237]
>
> [I climbed into the living room, only the moon stood and watched…and there was only a no from the dove's mouth, she crouched down and hugged herself then. We both burned blindly together. Then the fire died and glowed on the crane. My Heart lay red and rough and laughed.
>
> And love had her very much, she was my bride with all my heart. But this time all my joy came to an end: I bowed myself in gravel at her bidding, I prayed to her as I pray to God—all in vain...Damn, for misery, a pipe fire that never goes out!]

Clearly admitting his love for her, Svend also depicts a few transgressions on Iselin's part, if one believes he speaks truthfully. According to his statement, Svend will always have a feverish love for Iselin, whose actions do hint at reciprocation of this love. When Svend mentions that she hugged herself in the living room and crouched down while telling him no, Svend depicts a woman who states she does not want to partake in any act with Svend but secretly longs for it. Then, in his allusion to burning together blindly with her and that she was his bride, he alludes to an act that makes them secret lovers, possibly not the bride in his life but one in his heart. Svend reveals a transgression against the marriage between Didrik and Iselin, yet through the creative phrasing of his words, Svend can admit to it with the freedom of having his audience discredit the validity of his words. Furthermore, through this freedom, he conveys the truth and masks it with poetic imagery. Yet, he also speaks of the love that occurs at the wrong time and wrong place.

In the last monologue as an elderly person, Svend pieces together different imagery but cleverly masks his feelings about Iselin, as he begins to feel its effects more. While initially alluding to the nighttime during spring, he asks "Hvad--venter du Stilhed i Natters Tide naar Vaaren og Livet gryr?"[238] [What do you expect silence in the night time when spring and life are dawning?] followed by his reason for asking that "Det direr af

Kampe saa vid tog vide som Dyr monne møde Dyr."[239] [It vibrates with battles as far and wide as animals can meet animals.] After mentioning that a wanderer comes to reap up the benefits—an allusion to Munken Vendt made in his presence—he ends with a mysterious line to sum up his point: "Se, Natten er Livet og Kvinden dets Hersker, og Manden er Oksen i Verden som tærsker den Tone der aldrig dør"[240] "[Look, the night is life and the woman its ruler, and the man is the ox in the world that threshes the tone that never dies]." Then, he leaves to follow where Iselin left. In his last line, he resolves that life consists of women who will make up the rules though men continuously work through the repercussions of this rule, which include growth of grain. Here, Svend uses his imagery loosely as his allusions refer to love as a type of produce that women create, thus his poetic allusions refer to work.

If readers believe that Svend and Iselin do not partake in an amorous bond—social norms would not allow her to do so—then these poetic words are simply sublimated words that soften the blow of their inability to be together. Sublimation reframes the repressed feelings in order to protect the lovers, but in Hamsun's depiction, he allows it to persist in the poetic allusion. Considering that this affection between Svend and Iselin persists throughout the play despite consummation, it comes to life in the open every time Svend refers to it. Thus, it alludes to Zupančič's description of love in the Real as occurring in some other time and place, perhaps another dimension. Since Hamsun focuses on *Munken Vendt* as the main contributor of the theme through Munken's actions, monologues, and critique on religion, Iselin and Svend function as minor characters. Iselin only becomes important when readers surmise her relationship to Munken, as the one who experiences unreciprocated love yet desire from him. For this reason, the union between Svend and Iselin is left open to view without yet also ambiguous. Svend's words reinforce this paradoxical aspect: they reveal his feelings and hint at some transgression on both their parts but also conceal the validity as they are only poetic words. If a reader embraces this ambiguity as a minor idea in this play—Svend disappears after he follows Iselin, and Iselin dies when she discovers that Munken becomes injured—then, one might wonder at the possibilities if Iselin did show her reciprocated feelings or if Svend did not pull away when she did show favoritism towards him. Like Zupančič mentions, love in the Real cannot happen at the right time, a reason why a reader only perceives this love between them when disregarding the main interpretation of the play as Munken's journey of desire and transgression.

As a result, Iselin resolves the confusion caused by the seeming inconsistency in her characterization. Only through the lens of sublimation and the view of love between her and Svend can one perceive in the possibility that she is the same Iselin in *Pan*. Her depiction in *Pan* becomes the mythological version of her desired being in *Munken Vendt*. As Didrik witnesses a change in her being toward the end of the play, she transforms in her being by giving into her restlessness and reflecting on her "sins" that she committed yet does not explain further. While this view should not replace the dominant perspective of the play as a pastoral ironic tale of fateful transgression, it presents an explanation for the difference in depiction in Iselin's character while still providing an exploration for the possibility of the relationship between these depictions. When examining the two Iselins as the same character, I consider *Munken Vendt's* Iselin as the origin of *Pan*'s Iselin; she is mythological in both narratives, yet her strong convictions in *Munken Vendt* explain for her insistence to not leave the forest and to lure future hunters. Furthermore, her ability to incite poetic stories in all of Hamsun's iterations of her character reflect a consistency in the depiction of her character.

With this assessment, I resolve the tension that sometimes presents itself in academic articles, and in doing so, I finally attempt to solve the case I was given years ago. Unfortunately, I also had no idea that I had to resolve this particular case, the incongruency between Iselin's character in *Pan* and Iselin's character in *Munken Vendt*. I thought I had to explore other cases, but this is in fact the case that I was given years ago in a dream with the shoes. Like many cases involving literary analysis, investigators take different approaches and reveal various perspectives, but for me, this particular case resonates more than just my fascination with Hamsun's earlier work. It was the first case that proved the necessity of using intuition within my reasoning. This method provided a way to rectify the more creative process of sensing a perspective with my use of logical ability to reason with the different arguments. Nonetheless, I close this case with the understanding that a myriad of smaller cases seeks my method of resolution.

Illustration: The Red Beret

Chapter 8

Making the Impossible Happen

> When we love something, we mythologize it. We soften its weaknesses and eliminate its deficiencies. We highlight its beauty. Its gaze over us blinds our vision when we create an artifact to construct a concrete version of it. Yet, the result is the same; nothing ever truly captures our desire or experience of it. Due to this failure of image and words, we persist to capture and recapture precisely because it sustains our bond to it.
>
> Lisa Yamasaki

> "The Real is not a specifiable object endowed with laws of movement on its own, but, on the contrary, something that only exists and shows itself through its disruptive effects within the Symbolic." (Ernesto Laclau as quoted in Caleb Cates, M. Lane Bruner, and Joseph T. Moss III 2018, 152)

During a recent presentation on Norwegian authors, I was asked a question about the way that I became involved with Nordic authors and culture as opposed to the content in my presentation. Initially, I offered the answer in one word, as this phenomenon motivated me to continue reading, translating, contacting senior scholars on the topic, and researching perspectives during the time period in order to inform my writing. Despite having done all this work to provide the best foundation for my research, I understand that the story behind my interest that became my desired area of expertise compels people more than the actual research. And to better foreground the tale itself, which may embellish some details while hiding others, I present a myth to illustrate its parallels to my story.

My previous investigation on a video game series was successful, and one of its themes was based on the premise where a particularly sweet-tasting dessert was proven to be a lie. In this story, the dessert was the incentive for players to continue playing the game, and I had written about the dessert as a means of disguising the desire for death. Such darkness surrounded that inquiry, yet my analysis also predicted the façade of my ease in it or any initial promises of future success that I would have had. If I take this theme of the dessert as being that lie that all players must believe to continue their game, then it renders one's faith in the lie as useless. If the dessert were a lie, they will continue playing regardless of the outcome. And in the case of this game, the curiosity of seeing the story usually entertains the player. If such a premise is true—as indicated by the results of my previous investigation—then it must follow that its inverse might also be true. To put it clearly, if the dessert is a lie but one that others believe in order to continue playing the game, then it is possible that all stories we believe are fictional—legends, myths, fairytales, dreams—must have some element of truth.

In the process of reading a collection of Norwegian folktales, I find John Bierhorst's *Black Rainbow: Legends of the Incas and Myths of Ancient Peru*, a book on Peruvian legends, and in particular, one legend, "The Llama Herder and The Daughter of the Sun," interests me though not for its account of ill-fated love. Still, its intriguing tale warrants a description of its details. Romantic in nature, the legend chronicles a daughter of the sun who meets a llama herder and falls in love with him, and he with her. Due to her love for him, she cannot eat once she returns to the sun palace. Such crucial details include the woman's dream she has of a nightingale who instructs her to sing of her love in a fountain in the sun palace, and the fountain will repeat the words to her. Once she awakens, she heads to the fountain and sings the words, "suck, tick, move, heart, come,"[241] and the fountain sings them back to her. In doing so, this mirroring caused the sun's daughter to consider her love for him genuine and true, as it meant that he too harbored these feelings. The story follows that the llama herder becomes ill, and the sun daughter tries to cure him once she visits the earth. Then, she takes a staff back to her sun palace, only to find that the llama herder is hidden inside of it due to his mother's trickery. Nonetheless, the herder and the sun's daughter consummate their love for one another, yet they get discovered when they leave the sun palace. In other words, her love for him compels her to leave her home. When a guard of the sun palace discovers them and follows them on earth, they get turned into two peaks in the mountain, Pitsusiray.[242] To this day, this actual mountain symbolizes feminine and masculine energy. Though the detail about the dream and the nightingale are fascinating, I am more curious about the legend's mention of two daughters coming down from the sun. The sun's daughter, Chuquillantro, who falls in love with the herder, had a younger sister. At some point, the legend states that she is no longer be mentioned due to her insignificance to the story. Several versions of this legend state precisely the same information: she is no longer relevant. She was only present to accompany her sister and to witness the love between her sister and the herder. Due to the lack of details In regard to her character as well as the strong focus on Chuquillantro's perspective, one cannot discern what happens to her sister even though one might assume that she maintains her existence as a daughter of the sun unlike her sister. Though I do not explore these legends further, I do wonder what happened to the other daughter of the sun.

Since legends and myths possess an element of historical value, they are part of a culture's distinctive beliefs and customs. While not everyone from a particular culture adheres to the same beliefs, the legends, myths, and fairytales provide additional insights to others to better understand the culture at hand. Even in the omission of a particular character, one gains the understanding that the legend explains for the existence of a particular mountain range, so any other outlying detail outside of the couple who eventually form the mountain range is superfluous.

I once believed that when one experiences a profound feeling or event, one then tells and retells the story, creating a myth about the experience until the storyteller's own understanding of the event or feeling changes. Some details become embellished, while others dim in significance. Nonetheless, the storyteller accepts this mythologized version, consciously or not. These minor omissions, however, suggest that any further telling of the minor details, such as the whereabouts of the younger sister in the Peruvian legend, would deviate from the story. One might define a deviation as a departure of a given standard, rules, and expectations: an interruption that disrupts the usual events. The natural inclination is to disregard these interruptions and deviations before omitting them from story. I question what happens when one does listen to the interruption and follows the path formed by the disruptive details of a story. Does it allow for a new set of standards and expectations, or does one simply regard it as a rupture that one releases into poetic hypotheticals?

So, when I was asked how I started my work in Nordic literature, I had to quickly develop an accurate account of the main events that formed my decision to abandon my other research and engage in research on nineteenth century Norwegian literature. While the other panelists did not have any questions about my work, they expressed interest about my path into Nordic studies without any regard to the work I had done previously. Upon reflection of this story, I recount the following myth based on real events:

> When accepting entry into my doctoral program, I went into a well-known public research university with the specific goal to establish a new educational philosophy that focuses on the teacher-student intersubjectivity phenomenon. Such an investigation entailed looking into the teacher's subjectivity as well as the student's subjectivity, and I needed to gain more expertise into psychoanalytic ideas and further elaborate my knowledge in this area. Consequently, I learned that such an abstract and philosophical path on a mission that entailed more hands-on experience was neither fruitful nor approved by the majority of the department. Across the country, many philosophical divisions within education were closing and diminishing. After discussing my concerns with different faculty members and my observation on the increasingly popular use of digital media and video games in learning environments, I decided to change direction. Contributing to my mentor's discussion of critical media literacy would guarantee success, as my research would only add the component of video games in the larger discussion of learning critically through media representation.

So far, this story sounds like a typical demystifying process of acclimating into the academic world from a master's program onto a doctoral program, where much emphasis is placed on strategy and foresight. Yet, I offset this plan by accidentally responding to an email.

After my data collection resulted in data analysis for my first investigation, I received an email to being a teaching assistant for academic writing classes in a literature department. Since I did take some classes in writing pedagogy, I had the qualifications to teach the class, though I was a bit unfamiliar with the literature. On a whim, I responded to it and submitted my resume and qualifications. Though I was not hired that summer, I did get an email asking about my interest during early fall of that year.

While I edited the analysis of my investigation on a video game, I absorbed the information in the classes I taught. Though I was only meant to be a hire for the fall quarter, I was asked to continue onto the following quarter and then to finish the year. Some of the students from external departments, like myself, moved on from their assignment and graduated. During my second year as a teaching assistant, I was finalizing my analysis from my investigation and had a feeling that it would be my last year. After all, I had fulfilled my purpose and the added bonus of teaching experience gave me the confidence to start applying to jobs. It was a wonderful detour I was taking, but I needed to use the upcoming summer to work on postdoctoral applications for other investigations of different video game narratives.

But one day in 2015, I sat with my co-teaching assistants and smiled at ease, as I took notes on the lecture on Knut Hamsun's *Hunger*. *Oh goodness, this book again*, I thought to myself. *This book just chronicles one starving artist's inability to write and love with a minimal plot. I just have to push past this book and anticipate the next book in this class*. I looked at the presentation slide with a picture of young Hamsun with a monocle. He smiled at everyone in the audience, as if he were pleased that the book that he had suffered to write would eventually become required reading at the university level. Just before the class ended, however, I heard a slight reverberation of a whispered voice to reread the book carefully. Perhaps I had missed a detail the first time I read it and had made an error in judgment. I could have dismissed this whisper as a fanciful notion or logically explained it as an utterance from my peers. Instead, I chose to believe in my initial interpretation of the whisper as such and smiled at my co-teaching assistants as we offered each other good luck for our upcoming classes.

I was supposed to read *Hunger* and then move on and apply to other jobs. But once I found his short novel, *Victoria*, I could not move onto my plans. I spent the spring reading a list of books that would eventually form the reading list for my summer class that I taught as the instructor.

Eventually, I did graduate with my doctorate. The plan was to turn that first investigation into a formal report and attain other positions where I would work with a mentor on other investigations similar in nature—investigating the video game narratives in other games. But in my plans to execute that goal, I wrote the supplementary material without any foresight into the way that the opportunities might enhance my future. Nonetheless, my proposals were adequate; I snuck in some more reading of the Scandinavian authors, specifically Hamsun's *Pan*. While I would force myself to research a few games that would explore psychological concepts, I longed for the times when I indulged in other reading material, where the worlds permeated into my own. I realized that the past couple of years of studying narratives based on binary code had cheapened the idea of narrative; once I stepped into passages of nineteenth century text where scenes of a man's search for love matches the rosy haze in the summer sky, I recognized that I allowed myself to envision a world that elicited my innate understanding. I stepped into a world of painting through text, one that I could see since I was a painter but also an analyst. The more I tried to repress these disruptions and ignore them, the more I puzzled at the timing of failed opportunities that made my original plan a failure.

After the second summer of teaching, I had a moment-changing conversation with a new mentor who showed genuine sympathy and compassion. After our conversation, I acknowledged that I had two paths set before me, both meandering with their own dark shrubbery yet separate from one another. They would never meet at a clearing in the distant future. One path revealed the choice to pursue older literature and obtain an adequate level of Norwegian to help me translate the old Dano-Norwegian text, while the other offered me the opportunity to further develop my understanding of video games, narratives built by binary code. By engaging with the binary code systems, I would learn more about game mechanics to curb my instinct to find narrative in everything; I would strengthen the write-up of the final report by digging deeper into game mechanics and join the group of growing scholars who talked about this artifact. I would also continue looking at representation of characters and secure the legacy of my previous mentor. This path, however, would forever block my entry into exploring the passages of paintings through text. Through these powerful scenes, I understood the way that certain male figures sublimated, the way that their craft and storytelling sparked with the same impulse one finds in love. Even past and present American authors—brilliant as they are—did not elicit this same understanding within me; I finally found it in Nordic text. Yet, I would forfeit all this exploration if I chose to study binary code, the new frontier.

I chose life.

Running down that dark meandering path required that I initially feel my way around the trees and thick branches before I analyze. I needed to carefully watch my step. At times, the abundant sunlight showed me ways to prance around different walkways among the line of trees, as the extended days enhanced my vision. In taking this path, I also had to prepare myself in those days

> where the sun did not come up at all. Instead of giving into fear, I learned to adjust my sight. Though I did sometimes fall into traps that were initially covered by dirt and fallen branches, I used my strength to pull myself out of them. This path showed up at the wrong place and time; perhaps it was intended for an American woman from the late nineteenth century.

Thus, this myth explains how the impossible happens: a disruption in the main path supplants that same path for set of numerous possibilities. Instead of focusing on the intended way out of the woods, I uncover the small details, the flowering of a blossom in spring or the charming change in the direction of the sun in autumn. I note its details in writing and in drawing as the combination of the two encapsulate a narrative informed by symbolic significance, distinct imagery, and the enigma of the unexplainable. Though I do choose a particular way to analyze the literature I have chosen to examine, I treat them as these moments where the stories present different ways of seeing aspects of life. In the previous chapters, I discuss narratives of trauma but also prophetic daydreams. While they contrast to the theme of sublimation that I covered in the majority of this book, they are related in that they are part of the overarching method I have used throughout this process: an exploration of seemingly insignificant disruptions from the main narrative as they appear in dreams and bizarre behavioral impulses. When examining these small parts of the text, I recognize their significance to the whole narrative.

Illustration: Little Spring Bouquet

Illustration: Tree in Fog

Illustration: Teacup

Chapter 9

The Last Dream

A woman sees me walking up a long walkway to a dark house. The air is chilly, like that time when I was in Norway. I zip up my jacket to better contain my body heat. The house is two-story with light trimming and a high pointed roof, like the ones I used to draw as a kid.

The door opens without having me turn the doorknob. A light comes in, as I walk inside the house and accompanies me as I approach a woman who stands in the middle of the living room and greets me warmly. It's the same woman from that first dream, only now she smiles as me as a welcomed guest. This time her hair is pulled up in a loose bun, and she wears a long dark dress.

I look around and see that the kitchen is tidy and clean but hot as if the oven had been turned on. A tea kettle rests on the stove, and I do not notice whether steam rises from it. Still, the woman brings a cup to me. Though I should be cautious—a woman brings me a cup of a liquid whose contents I am not aware of. I take a sip—hmm, chamomile.

As it is always the case with older nineteenth century people, she looks at my face and hair and remarks how lovely it is. *How the future holds such eccentric people yet so familiar to us at the same time.* She says it, and it aptly defines the look on the faces from people in the past. Before the automobile, people traveled less frequently and did not get a chance to relocate as compared to now. For the past couple of generations, my family moved to different countries, carrying their last names that always make people question their country of origin. While I am someone who loves the melting pot that characterizes America, I finally wonder if I am meant to emigrate to Norway.

I wander upstairs and look at the simple décor, just a few paintings in the hallway. A few small bedrooms and a bathroom. There is a small window at the end of the hallway, and the sun casts its light onto that space on the landing. Though there is no furniture there yet, I imagine how it would be perfect for a reading nook. I feel myself pulling away from this house, as the light forces me to open my eyes.

No, not yet.

I walk downstairs and find the woman still waiting for me. Is this dream somehow more meaningful as it refuses to shift and change until I get its intention?

I hand her my cup that I have finished. After putting it aside on the kitchen counter, she grabs my hands and firmly grasps them. Though I might be frightened in usual situations where this would normally arise, I am not in this particular meeting.

"I know he would have wanted you to stay here to work on the book," she tells me. "Had he lived long enough to see you. I will give you the key for whenever you are ready to come here and work. This place is yours. It doesn't have to be today or tomorrow, but whenever you are ready and find work here, you have a place to stay. He would have wanted it to be that way."

I do not ask her to whom she refers. We both know. She says something else that alarms me yet validates the other dreams I have had as truth—it is the only way that all those dreams in the succession that they occurred make sense. She nods as a gesture indicating for me to accept her words, as I feel tears stream down my face. I do not know why I cry, but it might have to do with the fact that I want to believe in what she says. I feel the immense sunlight fill the room, and I open my eyes to find myself return to my waking life. The only remaining part of the dream is the sunlight now breaking free in my room. It fills the room with immense heat.

Within a few months, I decide to pause my teaching. With the exception of a few students, the most claim that their minds fogged up when reading the older literature. They could see the words just fine, but when they would try to understand them they could only see the literature in context to recent iterations of similar storylines and characters. They would not see the names of the characters nor the storylines in the nineteenth century context, but rather the settings within an Americanized context. Some only understood the most current literature about dysfunctional relationships and the dead dreams of idealism, while others devoted their time to the entanglement of humans and machines. Only a handful could perceive the images from the words that the older literature depicted. And I, too defensive over the wishes of the ghosts, realized that it was better to leave the young to their disheartened illusions than to delineate the poetic imagery of the older literature. Thus, my failure of my teaching profession originates from my love for the writers and their words, and perhaps, my love is only beginning to extend to the peers of the authors I have written about.

I believe that analysts are selected by their objects of study, and not the other way around. If I am to understand the works of these writers, I constantly navigate between my known American world to that of the Norwegian past. When I say, "Unnskyld," as a way to pardon any interruption or disruption as to the flow of events, the corresponding meaning of the sound of that word in English do not escape me. It comes up when I seek to excuse my obstinance for defending the ghosts. "Un" and "shield." I sometimes wonder if I mean to say "Disarm yourself: I mean no harm." I do not mean to hurt anyone with my insistence that we continue to study the works of these men, so I request that anyone disarm themselves.

The best way to defend what one loves is to not speak of it. When people now ask me what I am passionate about, I always say "Norwegian literature" but do not qualify which authors I read the most. Americans generally do not ask for further details; they simply nod and smile. I do not tell them that this literature moves me to forget my previous preoccupations with ideas that I thought would give me a favorable reputation as an academic. I leave aside that old document where I had once written my educational philosophy that would change the way schools would regard students and teachers. I cast aside my concern as to whether I am contributing any new ideas as a Lacanian, or if I should define myself that way even though it is an accurate term for me. I am happy in the Symbolic; I drop my pretenses about being relevant in the field and pursuing the Real. If I am in the age where I have no time to lie to myself, I must say that I only liked the Real when I thought that exploring it would bring everyone closer to their true actualized selves.

I only have time to focus on the present, though the present consists of going back into the past. I protect the past and remain in my armor, but I am slightly bothered that I do not know where this preoccupation leads me. I wish I could say that it would take me to Norway, the way I once thought back in 2019. Though I will find my way back, I do not know whether I should worry about the path, but more so how I know what skills will best suit what I am becoming. I feel a heaviness, either due to the ethical responsibility for playing detective on a provocative and controversial writer or my own stubbornness. I am compelled to continue exploring the literary themes of a writer whose unconscious betrayed him.

For now, I remain open, yet standing guard at the particular clearing in the woods, not the deep heavily forested area, but more like a forest within a city.

Illustration: The White Rose

Illustration: The Open Door

Endnotes

Introduction

[1] Sigmund Freud, "The Uncanny," in *The Standard Edition of the Complete Psychological Works of Sigmund Freud,* Trans. James Strachey (London: The Hogarth Press, 1925), 224.
[2] Knut Hamsun, "Unconscious Life of the Mind," in *Acta Nordica Studier i språk- og litteraturevitenskap.* Eds. Ståle Dingstad, Ylva Frød, Elisabeth Oxfeldt, and Ellen Rees, (Cambridge: Tapic Academic Press, 2011), 281-289.
[3] Hamsun, "Unconscious Life of the Mind," 286-287.
[4] Hamsun, "Unconscious Life of the Mind," 283.
[5] Hamsun, "Unconscious Life of the Mind," 288.
[6] Hamsun, "Unconscious Life of the Mind," 288.
[7] Hamsun, "Unconscious Life of the Mind," 288.
[8] Sigmund Freud, *The Interpretation of Dreams*, trans. and ed. James Strachey (New York: Basic Books, 2010) 147.
[9] Freud, *The Interpretation of Dreams*, 159.
[10] Carl Nærup. *Illustretet Norsk Litteraturshistorie.* (Kristiania: Det Norske Akiteforlang, 1905), 182.
[11] Nærup, *Illustretet Norsk Litteraturshistorie,* 182.
[12] Nærup, *Illustretet Norsk Litteraturshistorie,* 182.
[13] Sigmund Freud, "The Uncanny," in *The Standard Edition of the Complete Psychological Works of Sigmund Freud,* Trans. James Strachey (London: The Hogarth Press, 1925), 236.
[14] Harald Næss, "George Brandes and 19th Century Scandinavian Realism" in *Neohelicon* 15, no. 2 (1988): 132.
[15] Pirjo Lyytikäinen, Riikka Rossi, Viola Parente-Čapková, Mirjam Hinrikus, *Nordic Literature of Decadence* (New York and Milton Park: Routledge, 2020) para. 29.
[16] Pirjo Lyytikäinen, Riikka Rossi, Viola Parente-Čapková, Mirjam Hinrikus, *Nordic Literature of Decadence*, para. 31.
[17] Pirjo Lyytikäinen, Riikka Rossi, Viola Parente-Čapková, Mirjam Hinrikus, *Nordic Literature of Decadence*, para. 38.
[18] Kjersti Bale, "Melancholy at a Crossroads: Effeminate Men in Norwegian Fin-de-siècle Literature." *Scandinavian Studies* 93, no. 3 (2021): 377.

[19] Pirjo Lyytikäinen, Riikka Rossi, Viola Parente-Čapková, Mirjam Hinrikus, *Nordic Literature of Decadence* (New York and Milton Park: Routledge, 2020) para. 47.
[20] Pirjo Lyytikäinen, Riikka Rossi, Viola Parente-Čapková, Mirjam Hinrikus, *Nordic Literature of Decadence*, para. 57.
[21] John Bramble, *Modernism and the Occult* (London: Palgrave Macmillan, 2015) 6.
[22] Bramble, *Modernism and the Occult*, 23-25.
[23] Ola Hansson, *Sensitiva Amorosa.* Trans. Paul Norlen. (Wisconsin: Department of Scandinavian Studies University of Wisconsin, 2002) 33.
[24] Hansson, *Sensitiva Amorosa*, 33.
[25] Hansson, *Sensitiva Amorosa*, 34.
[26] Hansson, *Sensitiva Amorosa*, 34.
[27] Hansson, *Sensitiva Amorosa*, 34.
[28] Hansson, *Sensitiva Amorosa*, 34.
[29] Stefano Evangelista. "The Time of Ola Hansson: Translating Scandinavian Decadence in fin de siècle France and England," *Nordic Literature of Decadence.* Ed. Pirjo Lyytikäinen, Riikka Rossi, Viola Parente-Čapková, and Mirjam Hinrikus (New York: Routledge, 2020) para. 11.
[30] Pirjo Lyytikäinen, Riikka Rossi, Viola Parente-Čapková, Mirjam Hinrikus, *Nordic Literature of Decadence* (New York and Milton Park: Routledge, 2020) para. 30.
[31] Tzvetan Todorov, *The Fantastic: A Structural Approach to a Literary Genre.* Trans. Richard Howard (Cleveland/London: The Press of Case Western Reserve University, 1973) 52.
[32] Todorov, *The Fantastic: A Structural Approach to a Literary Genre*, 33.
[33] Todorov, *The Fantastic: A Structural Approach to a Literary Genre*, 41.
[34] Avery F. Gordon, *Ghostly Matters: Haunting and the Sociological Imagination* (Minneapolis: University of Minnesota Press, 2008) 95.
[35] Gordon, *Ghostly Matters: Haunting and the Sociological Imagination,* 108.
[36] Deleuze, Gilles. *Difference and Repetition.* Trans. Paul Patton. (New York: Columbia University Press, 1994) 85.
[37] Marcel Proust. *In Search of Lost Time: Swann's Way*, Trans. C.K. Scott Moncrieff and Terence Kilmartin (New York: The Modern Library, 2003) 59.
[38] Proust, *In Search of Lost Time: Swann's Way*, 59.
[39] Proust, *In Search of Lost Time: Swann's Way*, 60.

Chapter 1

[40] Knut Hamsun, *Pan: Av Løitnant Thomas Glahns Papirer*, (Oslo: Glydendal Norsk Forlag, 1968), 33.
[41] Jacques Lacan, "Seminar on 'The Purloined Letter'" in *Ecrits.* Trans. Bruce Fink (New York and London: W.W. Norton & Company, 2006) 17.

[42] Jacques Lacan, "Field and Function of Speech and Language in Psychoanalysis," in *Ecrits*. Trans. Bruce Fink (New York and London: W.W. Norton & Company Inc, 2006) 231.
[43] Monika Žagar, *The Dark Side of Literary Brilliance* (Seattle: University of Washington Press, 2009) 176.
[44] Monika Žagar, *The Dark Side of Literary Brilliance,* 162.
[45] Monika Žagar, *The Dark Side of Literary Brilliance,* 110.
[46] J.W. McFarlane, "The Whisper of the Blood: A Study of Knut Hamsun's Early Novels," *Modern Language Association* 71, no. 4 (1956): 591.
[47] Dean Krouk, "Prophet of Regeneration: On Two Fascist Readings of Knut Hamsun" in *Nordlit,* 25, Juni (2010): 33.
[48] Dean Krouk, "Prophet of Regeneration: On Two Fascist Readings of Knut Hamsun," 32.
[49] J.W. McFarlane, "The Whisper of the Blood: A Study of Knut Hamsun's Early Novels," *Modern Language Association* 71, no. 4 (1956): 568-69.

Chapter 2

[50] Even Arntzen, "Munken Vendt—På Sporet av Knut Hamsuns Mytiske Esteikk." In *Hamsun i Tromsø. 11 Foredraf fra Hamsun-konferansen i Tromsø 1995,* ed. N.M. Knutsen (Tromsø: Hamsun-Selskapet,1996) 100.
[51] Even Arntzen,"Munken Vendt—På Sporet av Knut Hamsuns Mytiske Esteikk," 100-101.
[52] Monika Žagar, *The Dark Side of Literary Brilliance* (Seattle: University of Washington Press, 2009) 10-11.
[53] Arne Lunde, "Politics, Aesthetics, and Afterlife in På gjengrodde stier: Retracing Knut Hamsun's 'Overgrown Paths' Toward Nazism." In *Scandinaviaca* 47, no. 2 (2008): 180.
[54] Pål Bjørby, "Eros and Subjectivity: Knut Hamsun's Pan and Ragnhild Jølsen's Rikka Gan." In *Fin(s) de Siècle in Scandinavian perspective: Studies in Honor of Harald S. Naess*, ed. Faith Ingwersen and Mary Kay Norseng (New York: Camden House, 1993) 127.
[55] Antoine Faivre, *Western esotericism: a concise history*. (New York: Suny Press, 2010) 10-11.
[56] Frode Lerum Boasson, "Reaksjonær radikalisme Hamsuns vitalistiske poetikk." *Nordlit* 38 (April 2016): 79-80.
[57] Frode Lerum Boasson, "Men Livet lever: Hamsuns vitalisme fra Pan til Ringen Sluttet." (PhD diss, Norges teknisk naturvitenskalelig universitet, 2015) 85.
[58] Frode Lerum Boasson, "Reaksjonær radikalisme Hamsuns vitalistiske poetikk," 83.

[59] Sigmund Freud. “On Narcissism,” in *The Freud Reader*, ed. Peter Gay. (New York: W.W. Norton & Co. Inc, 1989) 598.
[60] Ken Germes, “Freud and Nietzsche on Sublimation.” *Journal of Nietzsche Studies* 39, no. Fall (2009): 41.
[61] In his essay, “Repression,” Freud defines repression as an impulsive act within the unconscious that rejects a stimulus. This energy remains in the unconscious and involves turning a representation of an instinct away from conscious activity. Repression involves ideational representations of a particular stimulus and a need to release the drive, yet sublimation turns it into an object within the self (see Freud 1989). In *Ego and the Id*, Freud (1960) formulates the way that it becomes incorporated into the ego-ideal and substantiates his previous claim in his essay, “Repression.” While sublimation is not part of what creates the ego-ideal, it does involve sublimation in so far as it involves abandoning object-cathexis and the first identification with a person (which Freud called the Oedipal Complex). According to Germes,The creation of the ego-ideal shows a mastery of the Oedipal Complex and has its subjection to the id, what Loewald defines as the defense (see Germes for more information).
[62] Jacques Lacan, *The Ethics of Psychoanalysis 1959-1960*. Trans. Dennis Porter (New York and London: W.W. Norton & Company, Inc, 1986) 293.
[63] Sigmund Freud. *Ego and the Id.* Ed. Peter Gay (New York: W.W. Norton & Company, Inc, 1960) 25.
[64] Jacques Lacan, *The Ethics of Psychoanalysis 1959-1960*, 148-150.
[65] Jacques Lacan, *The Ethics of Psychoanalysis 1959-1960*, 140.
[66] Jacques Lacan, *The Ethics of Psychoanalysis 1959-1960*, 150.
[67] Henning Howlid Wærp, “Knut Hamsun’s *Pan*: Nordlandsnatur eller Symbollandskap?” in Hele Livet en Vandrer i Nature: Økokristiske Lesninger i Knut Hamsuns Forfatterskap (Stamsund: Orkana Akademisk, 2018) 131.
[68] Knut Hamsun, *Pan: Av Løitnant Thomas Glahns Papirer*. (Oslo: Glydendal Norsk Forlag, 1968) 18.
[69] Knut Hamsun, *Pan: Av Løitnant Thomas Glahns Papirer*, 47.
[70] Knut Hamsun, *Pan: Av Løitnant Thomas Glahns Papirer*, 47.
[71] Knut Hamsun, *Pan: Av Løitnant Thomas Glahns Papirer*, 47.
[72] Knut Hamsun, *Pan: Av Løitnant Thomas Glahns Papirer*, 48.
[73] Dolores. Buttry “Avatar of Transgression: Hamsun’s Munken Vendt.” *Nordlit* 13, no. 2 (2009): 223.
[74] Even Arntzen, “Munken Vendt—På Sporet av Knut Hamsuns Mytiske Esteikk,” 100.
[75] Jacques Lacan, *The Ethics of Psychoanalysis 1959-1960*, 238.

[76] Jacques Lacan. *Desire and Its Interpretations.* Trans. Cormac Gallagher. (www.lacaninireland.com, 2018) 58.
[77] Jacques Lacan, *The Four Fundamental Concepts of Psychoanalysis.* Trans. Alan Sheridan (New York and London: W.W. Norton & Company Inc, 1998) 256.
[78] Jacques Lacan, "Field and Function of Speech and Language in Psychoanalysis," In *Ecrits.* Trans. Bruce Fink (New York and London: W.W. Norton & Company Inc, 2006) 256.
[79] Stefanie von Schnurbein. "Knut Hamsun's Narrative Fetishism," in *Acta Nordica Studier i språk-og litteraturevitenskap.* Ed. Ståle Dingstad, Ylva Frød, Elisabeth Oxfeldt, and Ellen Rees (Tapic Academic Press, 2011) 50.
[80] Knut Hamsun, *Pan: Av Løitnant Thomas Glahns Papirer*, 18.
[81] Knut Hamsun, *Pan: Av Løitnant Thomas Glahns Papirer*, 48-50.
[82] As an aside, Glahn's choice of nature over Edvarda affirms Hamsun's vitalistic goals, as man's closeness to nature strengthens his vitalistic impulse. Inherent in my argument is the idea that Glahn achieves a proximity to his desire by encountering Iselin in nature. Boasson (see Boasson 2016) further indicates that Hamsun's notion of vitalism incorporates a Romantic notion, one that attributes authenticity to nature, and the Schopenhauerian notion of humans as part of the will. Thus, Glahn's closeness to nature, the forest and Iselin, shows a connection between emphasis on creation in vitalism and the promise of creation in the libidinal impulse.
[83] Knut Hamsun, *Pan: Av Løitnant Thomas Glahns Papirer*, 63.
[84] Knut Hamsun, *Pan: Av Løitnant Thomas Glahns Papirer*, 18.
[85] Knut Hamsun, *Pan: Av Løitnant Thomas Glahns Papirer*, 50.
[86] Knut Hamsun, *Victoria.* (Oslo: Gyldendal Norsk Forlag, 1964) 70.
[87] Jacques Lacan, *The Ethics of Psychoanalysis 1959-1960*, 150-151.
[88] Joan Copjec, *Imagine There's No Woman* (Cambridge: MIT Press, 2004) 30.
[89] Jacques Lacan, *The Ethics of Psychoanalysis 1959-1960*, 113.
[90] Knut Hamsun, *Victoria.* (Oslo: Gyldendal Norsk Forlag, 1964) 44.
[91] Knut Hamsun, *Victoria*, 76.
[92] Knut Hamsun, *Victoria*, 24.
[93] Frode Lerum Boasson, "Reaksjonær radikalisme Hamsuns vitalistiske poetikk." *Nordlit* 38 (April 2016): 79, accessed February 1, 2020. doi: https://doi.org/10.7557/13.3754.
[94] Benjamin Bigelow, "The Voice of the Blood: Vitalism and the Acoustic in Knut Hamsun's *Pan* (1894)," *Scandinavian Studies* 90, no. 4 (2018): 536. (For more details, also see Bigelow's dissertation "The Life of the

Soul: Vitalism and the Invisible in the Norwegian Fin de Siècle," University of Berkeley, 2017.)
[95] Dolores Buttry. "Avatar of Transgression: Hamsun's Munken Vendt." *Nordlit* 13, no. 2 (2009): 223.
[96] Dolores Buttry. "Avatar of Transgression: Hamsun's Munken Vendt," 223.
[97] Stefanie von Schnurbein. "Knut Hamsun's Narrative Fetishism," in *Acta Nordica Studier i språk-og litteraturevitenskap*. Ed. Ståle Dingstad, Ylva Frød, Elisabeth Oxfeldt, and Ellen Rees (Tapic Academic Press, 2011) 59.
[98] Stefanie von Schnurbein. "Knut Hamsun's Narrative Fetishism," 59.
[99] Stefanie von Schnurbein. "Knut Hamsun's Narrative Fetishism," 62.
[100] Jan Sjåvik. "Triangular Structures in Knut Hamsun's 'Pan," in *Pacific Coast Philology* 27, no.1/2, (1992): 118-119.
[101] Alexandra Columban, "Myths of Literary Creativity in Knut Hamsun's Hunger (1890) and Pan, from Lieutenant Thomas Glahn's Papers (1894)," in *Philologia* 56, no. 3 (2011): 206.
[102] Dolores Buttry. "The Muse and the Mimosa: Knut Hamsun's Portrayal of the Inspired Artist," *Germanic Notes and Reviews* 40, no. 1 (2009): 12.
[103] Jacques Lacan, *The Ethics of Psychoanalysis 1959-1960*, 163.

Chapter 3

[104] Sigmund Freud, "On Narcissism," in *The Freud Reader*, ed. Peter Gay, (New York: W.W. Norton & Co. Inc, 1989) 558.
[105] Hans W Loewald, *Sublimation: Inquiries into Theoretical Psychoanalysis* (New Haven: Yale University Press, 1988) 42.
[106] *Folktales of Norway*. Ed. Reidar Christiansen. Trans. Pat Shaw Iversen. (University of Chicago Press, Chicago and London, 1964) 260.
[107] Knut Hamsun, *Mysterier*, (Oslo: Gyldendal Norsk Forlag, 1954) 97.
[108] Knut Hamsun, *Mysterier*, 52.
[109] Atle Kittang, *Luft, Vind, Ingenging,* (Oslo: Gyldendal Norsk Forlag, 1984) 86.
[110] Atle Kittang, *Luft, Vind, Ingenging*, 84.
[111] Knut Hamsun, *Mysterier*, 55.
[112] Atle Kittang, *Luft, Vind, Ingenging*, 86.
[113] Henning Howlid Wærp, "Grenselinjen mellom hendelse og drøm" in *Hele Livet en Vandrer i Nature: Økokristiske Lesninger i Knut Hamsuns Forfatterskap* (Stamsund: Orkana Akademisk, 2018) 108-113.
[114] Jacques Lacan, *The Four Fundamental Concepts of Psychoanalysis.* Trans. Alan Sheridan (New York and London: W.W. Norton & Company Inc, 1998) 211.
[115] Atle Kittang, *Luft, Vind, Ingenging*, 92.

[116] Dolores Buttry. "The Muse and the Mimosa: Knut Hamsun's Portrayal of the Inspired Artist," *Germanic Notes and Reviews* 40, no. 1 (2009): 11.
[117] Ingar Sletten Kolloen, *Knut Hamsun: Dreamer and Dissenter,* Trans. Deborah Dawkin & Erik Skuggevik (New Haven: Yale University Press, 2009) 87.
[118] Ingar Sletten Kolloen, *Knut Hamsun: Dreamer and Dissenter,* 91.
[119] Knut Hamsun, *Mysterier*, 92.
[120] Knut Hamsun, *Mysterier*, 94.
[121] Knut Hamsun, *Mysterier*, 94.
[122] Jacques Lacan, *Freud's Papers on Technique 1953-1954*. Trans. John Forrester (New York and London: W.W. Norton & Company, Inc, 1991) 140.
[123] Atle Kittang, *Luft, Vind, Ingenging*, 86.
[124] Atle Kittang, *Luft, Vind, Ingenging*, 99.
[125] Atle Kittang, *Luft, Vind, Ingenging*, 99.
[126] Mladen Dolar, "'I Shall Be with you on Your Wedding-Night': Lacan and the Uncanny," in *October* 58, no. Autumn (1991): 12-13.
[127] Mladen Dolar, "'I Shall Be with you on Your Wedding-Night': Lacan and the Uncanny," 14.
[128] Knut Hamsun, *Mysterier*, 59.
[129] Knut Hamsun, *Mysterier*, 60.
[130] Knut Hamsun, *Mysterier*, 59.
[131] Knut Hamsun, *Mysterier*, 99.
[132] Knut Hamsun, *Mysterier*, 100.
[133] Jørgen Elbek, "The Nordic Nineties," in *Fin(s) de Siècle in Scandinavian perspective: Studies in Honor of Harald S. Næss.* Eds. Faith Ingwersen and Mary Kay Norseng, (Columbia: Camden House, 1993) 61.
[134] Jørgen Elbek. "The Nordic Nineties,"60.
[135] Michal Kruszelnicki. "Thomas Glahn and Johan Nagel: Towards the Abyss of Life's Tragic Indeterminacy," *Nordlit* 13, no. 2 (2010): 127-128.

Chapter 4

[136] Jacques Derrida & Bernard Stiegler, *The Spectralities Reader: Ghosts and Haunting in Contemporary Cultural Theory*, Eds. María del Pilar Blanco and Esther Peeren, (New York and London: Bloomsbury Academic, 2013) 5.
[137] Jacques Derrida, *Specters of Marx,* trans. Peggy Kamuf (New York and London: Routledge, 1994) 5.
[138] Jacques Derrida, *Specters of Marx,* trans. Peggy Kamuf (New York and London: Routledge, 1994) 6.
[139] Jacques Derrida & Bernard Stiegler, *The Spectralities Reader: Ghosts and Haunting in Contemporary Cultural Theory*, 42.
[140] Colin Davis, *Haunted Subjects: Deconstruction, Psychoanalysis and the Return of the Dead*, (New York: Palgrave Macmillan. 2007) 91.

[141] Roland Barthes, *Mythologies,* Trans. Annette Lavers (New York: Hill and Wang, 1972) 115.
[142] Roland Barthes, *Mythologies,* 109.
[143] Roland Barthes, *Mythologies,* 113.
[144] Roland Barthes, *Mythologies,* 128.
[145] Roland Barthes, *Mythologies,* 134.
[146] Cathy Caruth. *Unclaimed Experience: Trauma, Narrative, and History,* (Baltimore and London: John Hopkins University Press, 1996) 103.
[147] Davis, Colin. "État Présent: Hautology, Spectres and Phantoms," In *The Spectralities Reader: Ghosts and Haunting in Contemporary Cultural Theory,* eds. María del Pilar Blanco and Esther Peeren (New York and London: Bloomsbury Academic, 2013) 58.
[148] Jeffrey Andrew Weinstock, "from Introduction: The Spectral Turn," In *The Spectralities Reader: Ghosts and Haunting in Contemporary Cultural Theory,* eds. María del Pilar Blanco and Esther Peeren (New York and London: Bloomsbury Academic, 2013) 62.
[149] Julian Wolfreys, "from Preface: On Textual Haunting," in *The Spectralities Reader: Ghosts and Haunting in Contemporary Cultural Theory,* eds. María del Pilar Blanco and Esther Peeren (New York and London: Bloomsbury Academic, 2013) 71-72.

Chapter 5

[150] Knut Hamsun,"Dronningen av Saba," in *Samlede romancer og fortællinger,* (Kristiania og Køvenhavn: Gyldendalske Boghandel Nordisk Forlag, 1908) 28.
[151] Dolores Buttry. "Pursuit and Confrontation: The Short Stories of Knut Hamsun." *Scandinavian studies* 70, no. 2 (1998): 235.
[152] Ellen Rees. "Over-Determined Topography in Knut Hamsun's 'Dronningen Av Saba.'" *Scandinavian Studies* 80, no. 2 (2008): 192.
[153] Elisabeth Oxfeldt, *Nordic Orientalism: Paris and the Cosmopolitan Imagination 1800-1900* (Copenhagen: Museum Tusculanum Press University of Copenhagen, 2005) 206. See footnote 90 for more details.
[154] Elisabeth Oxfeldt, "Orientalism, Decadence and Ekphrasis in Hamsun's 'Dronningen av Saba,'" *Edda* 2 (2003): 182.
[155] Elisabeth Oxfeldt, "Orientalism, Decadence and Ekphrasis in Hamsun's 'Dronningen av Saba,'" 183.
[156] 1 Kings, 10: 7
[157] 1'Kings, 10: 9
[158] Elisabeth Oxfeldt, *Nordic Orientalism: Paris and the Cosmopolitan Imagination 1800-1900,* 210.
[159] Elisabeth Oxfeldt, *Nordic Orientalism: Paris and the Cosmopolitan Imagination 1800-1900,* 215.
[160] Knut Hamsun,"Dronningen av Saba," 14.

[161] Knut Hamsun,"Dronningen av Saba," 14.
[162] Mary Kay Norseng, *Sigbjørn Obstfelder* (Boston: Twayne Publishers, 1982) 93.
[163] Carl Nærup, *Illustretet Norsk Litteraturshistorie* (Kristiania: Det Norske Akiteforlang, 1905) 173.
[164] Sigbjørn Obstfelder, "Korset," *Skrifter II* (København: Glydendalske Boghandels Forlag, 1907) 72.
[165] Sigbjørn Obstfelder, "Korset," 71.
[166] Sigbjørn Obstfelder, "Korset," 73.
[167] Sigbjørn Obstfelder, "Korset," 72.
[168] Sigbjørn Obstfelder, "Korset," 100.
[169] Otto Reinert, "Ibsen and Mimesis," *Scandinavian Studies* 82, no. 2 (Summer 2010): 213.
[170] Robert Spoo, "Uncanny Returns in 'The Dead': Ibsenian Intertexts and the Estranged Infant," In *Joyce: The Return of the Repressed*, ed. Susan Stanford Friedman (Cornell University Press, 1993) 104.
[171] Otto Reinert, "Ibsen and Mimesis," 221.
[172] Sigbjørn Obstfelder, "Korset," 63-64.
[173] Sigbjørn Obstfelder, "Korset," 68.
[174] Sigbjørn Obstfelder, "Korset," 69.
[175] Henrik Ibsen, "Når Vi Døde Vågner," In *Samlede Værker, femte bind* (Kristiania og Køvenhavn: Glydendalske Boghandel Nordisk Forlag, 1907) Act I, 370.
[176] Henrik Ibsen, "Når Vi Døde Vågner," Act II, 391.
[177] Robert Spoo, "Uncanny Returns in 'The Dead': Ibsenian Intertexts and the Estranged Infant," 102.
[178] Frode Helland. "Irene: Objekt eller Subjekt?," in *Livet på Likstrå: Henrik Ibsens Når Vi Døde Vågner*. Ed.Lisbeth P. Wærp (Oslo: Landslaget for Norskundervisning og Cappelen Akademisk Forlag, 1999) 128.
[179] Per Buvik, "Kunsten, Kjønnet, og Kvinnen om Ibsens Når Vi Døde Vågner," in *Livet på Likstrå: Henrik Ibsens Når Vi Døde Vågner*. Ed. Lisbeth P. Wærp (Oslo: Landslaget for Norskundervisning og Cappelen Akademisk Forlag, 1999) 186.
[180] Alenka Zupančič, "On Love as Comedy," *Journal for Politics, Gender and Culture* 2, no. 2 (Summer 2003): 78.
[181] Henrik Ibsen, "Når Vi Døde Vågner," Act I, 379.
[182] Henrik Ibsen, "Når Vi Døde Vågner," Act I, 379.
[183] Henrik Ibsen, "Når Vi Døde Vågner," Act I, 379.
[184] Henrik Ibsen, "Når Vi Døde Vågner," Act II, 395.
[185] Henrik Ibsen, "Når Vi Døde Vågner," Act II, 402.
[186] Henrik Ibsen, "Når Vi Døde Vågner," Act III, 405.
[187] Henrik Ibsen, "Når Vi Døde Vågner," Act III, 411.
[188] Elinor Fuchs, "The Apocalyptic Ibsen: When We Dead Awaken," *Twentieth Century Literature* 46, no. 4 (2000): 397.
[189] Elinor Fuchs, "The Apocalyptic Ibsen: When We Dead Awaken," 398.

[190] Elinor Fuchs, "The Apocalyptic Ibsen: When We Dead Awaken," 398.
[191] Robert Spoo, "Uncanny Returns in 'The Dead': Ibsenian Intertexts and the Estranged Infant," 104.
[192] Robert Spoo, "Uncanny Returns in 'The Dead': Ibsenian Intertexts and the Estranged Infant," 103-104.
[193] Robert Spoo, "Uncanny Returns in 'The Dead': Ibsenian Intertexts and the Estranged Infant," 103.
[194] Frode Helland. "Irene: Objekt eller Subjekt?" 137.
[195] Per Buvik, "Kunsten, Kjønnet, og Kvinnen om Ibsens Når Vi Døde Vågner," 198.
[196] Beret Wicklund. "Kjønnskampens Kunst, Kunsten som Kjønnskamp," in *Livet på Likstrå: Henrik Ibsens Når Vi Døde Vågner.* Ed. Lisbeth P. Wærp (Oslo: Landslaget for Norskundervisning og Cappelen Akademisk Forlag, 1999) 213.

Chapter 6

[197] Per Buvik, "Kunsten, Kjønnet, og Kvinnen om Ibsens Når Vi Døde Vågner," in *Livet på Likstrå: Henrik Ibsens Når Vi Døde Vågner.* Ed. Lisbeth P. Wærp (Oslo: Landslaget for Norskundervisning og Cappelen Akademisk Forlag, 1999) 193.
[198] Frode Helland. "Irene: Objekt eller Subjekt?," in *Livet på Likstrå: Henrik Ibsens Når Vi Døde Vågner.* Ed.Lisbeth P. Wærp (Oslo: Landslaget for Norskundervisning og Cappelen Akademisk Forlag, 1999) 145-146.
[199] Sigmund Freud. "Medusa's Head," in *Writings on Art and Literature,* Edited by Werner Hamacher & David E. Wellbery (Stanford: Stanford University Press, 1997) 264-265.
[200] Susan R, Bowers, "Medusa and the Female Gaze," *NWSA Journal*, 2, no. 2 (Spring 1990): 217-235.
[201] Susan R, Bowers, "Medusa and the Female Gaze," 220-221.
[202] Susan R, Bowers, "Medusa and the Female Gaze," 222.
[203] Arthur A Miller. "An Interpretation of the Symbolism of Medusa." *American Imago* 15, no. 4 (Winter 1958): 396.
[204] Beret Wicklund. "Kjønnskampens Kunst, Kunsten som Kjønnskamp," in *Livet på Likstrå: Henrik Ibsens Når Vi Døde Vågner.* Ed. Lisbeth P. Wærp (Oslo: Landslaget for Norskundervisning og Cappelen Akademisk Forlag, 1999) 220.
[205] Hal Foster. "Medusa and the Real," *RES: Anthropology and Aesthetics*, No. 44 (August 2003): 189, 2003.
[206] Hal Foster. "Medusa and the Real," 190.
[207] Jacques Lacan, *The Four Fundamental Concepts of Psychoanalysis.* Trans. Alan Sheridan (New York and London: W.W. Norton & Company Inc, 1998) 73.
[208] Elisabeth Oxfeldt, "Orientalism, Decadence and Ekphrasis in Hamsun's 'Dronningen av Saba,'" *Edda* 2 (2003): 186.

[209] Jan Jagodzinski, "The Site/Cite of Jacques Lacan or Forget Slavoj Žižek? Implications for Art and Its Education," *Visual Arts Research* 36, no. 2 (Winter 2010): 29.

Chapter 7

[210] Alenka Zupančič, "On Love as Comedy," *Journal for Politics, Gender and Culture* 2, no. 2 (Summer 2003): 62.
[211] Alenka Zupančič, "On Love as Comedy," 72.
[212] Alenka Zupančič, "On Love as Comedy," 73.
[213] Alenka Zupančič, "On Love as Comedy," 78.
[214] Dolores. Buttry "Avatar of Transgression: Hamsun's Munken Vendt." *Nordlit* 13, no. 2 (2009): 223.
[215] Even Arntzen, "Munken Vendt—På Sporet av Knut Hamsuns Mytiske Esteikk." In *Hamsun i Tromsø. 11 Foredraf fra Hamsun-konferansen i Tromsø 1995,* ed. N.M. Knutsen (Tromsø: Hamsun-Selskapet,1996) 100-101.
[216] Knut Hamsun, *Munken Vendt,* (København: Gyldendalske Boghandel Nordisk Forlag (F. Hegel & Søn), 1902) 60.
[217] Knut Hamsun, *Munken Vendt*, 61.
[218] Knut Hamsun, *Munken Vendt*, 76.
[219] Knut Hamsun, *Munken Vendt*, 67.
[220] Knut Hamsun, *Munken Vendt*, 352.
[221] Knut Hamsun, *Munken Vendt*, 300.
[222] Knut Hamsun, *Munken Vendt*, 334.
[223] Knut Hamsun, *Munken Vendt*, 333.
[224] Alenka Zupančič, "On Love as Comedy," 74.
[225] Alenka Zupančič, "On Love as Comedy," 76-77.
[226] Alenka Zupančič, "On Love as Comedy," 74.
[227] Alenka Zupančič, "On Love as Comedy," 74.
[228] Alenka Zupančič, "On Love as Comedy," 74.
[229] Alenka Zupančič, "On Love as Comedy," 77.
[230] Josef Wiehr, *Knut Hamsun: His Personality and His Outlook upon Life* (Northampton and Paris: Smith College Studies in Modern Languages, 1922) 52.
[231] Josef Wiehr, *Knut Hamsun: His Personality and His Outlook upon Life*, 53.
[232] Knut Hamsun, *Munken Vendt*, 48.
[233] Knut Hamsun, *Munken Vendt*, 176.
[234] Knut Hamsun, *Munken Vendt*, 280.
[235] Knut Hamsun, *Munken Vendt*, 63-64.
[236] Knut Hamsun, *Munken Vendt*, 65.
[237] Knut Hamsun, *Munken Vendt*, 161.
[238] Knut Hamsun, *Munken Vendt*, 342.
[239] Knut Hamsun, *Munken Vendt*, 342.
[240] Knut Hamsun, *Munken Vendt*, 343.

Chapter 8

[241] John Bierhorst, *Black Rainbow: Legends of the Incas and Myths of Ancient Peru,* Trans. John Bierhorst (New York: Farrar, Straus, and Giroux, 1976) 53.
[242] John Bierhorst, *Black Rainbow: Legends of the Incas and Myths of Ancient Peru,* 57.

Bibliography

Bible entry—1 Kings, 10: 1-29. https://www.biblegateway.com/passage/?search=1+Kings+10&version=NIV

Folktales of Norway. Edited by Reidar Christiansen. Translated by Pat Shaw Iversen. University of Chicago Press, Chicago and London, 1964.

Arntzen, Even. "Munken Vendt—På Sporet av Knut Hamsuns Mytiske Esteikk." *Hamsun i Tromsø. 11 Foredraf fra Hamsun-konferansen i Tromsø 1995,* Edited by N.M. Knutsen, 94-105. Tromsø: Hamsun-Selskapet,1996.

Bale, Kjersti. "Melancholy at a Crossroads: Effeminate Men in Norwegian Fin-de-siècle Literature." *Scandinavian Studies* 93, no. 3 (2021): 357-382.

Barthes, Roland. *Mythologies.* Translated by Annette Lavers. New York: Hill and Wang, 1972.

Bauduin, Tessel M. & Johnsson, Henrik. *The occult in modernist art, literature, and cinema.* London: Palgrave Macmillan, 2018.

Beyer, Edvard. "Hamsun 1898-1912: Crisis of Regeneration," *Fin(s) de Siècle in Scandinavian perspective: Studies in Honor of Harald S. Naess.* Edited by Faith Ingwersen and Mary Kay Norseng. Columbia: Camden House, 1993.

Bierhorst, John. *Black Rainbow: Legends of the Incas and Myths of Ancient Peru.* Translated by John Bierhorst. New York: Farrar, Straus, and Giroux, 1976.

Bigelow, Benjamin. "The Voice of the Blood: Vitalism and the Acoustic in Knut Hamsun's *Pan* (1894)." *Scandinavian Studies* 90, no. 4 (2018): 531-552.

Bigelow, Benjamin. "The Life of the Soul: Vitalism and the Invisible in the Norwegian Fin de Siècle." PhD diss. University of California, Berkeley, 2017.

Bjørby, Pål. "Eros and Subjectivity: Knut Hamsun's Pan and Ragnhild Jølsen's Rikka Gan." In *Fin(s) de Siècle in Scandinavian perspective: Studies in Honor of Harald S. Naess*, Edited by Faith Ingwersen and Mary Kay Norseng, 123-140. New York: Camden House, 1993.

Boasson, Frode Lerum. "Reaksjonær radikalisme Hamsuns vitalistiske poetikk." *Nordlit* 38 (April 2016): 77-86.

Boasson, Frode Lerum. "Men Livet lever: Hamsuns vitalisme fra Pan til Ringen Sluttet." PhD diss. Norges teknisk naturvitenskalelig universitet, 2015.

Bowers, Susan R. "Medusa and the Female Gaze." *NWSA Journal*, 2, no. 2 (Spring 1990): 217-235.

Bramble, John. *Modernism and the Occult.* London: Palgrave Macmillan, 2015.

Buttry, Dolores. "Avatar of Transgression: Hamsun's Munken Vendt." *Nordlit* 13, no. 2 (2009): 219-38.

Buttry, Dolores. "The Muse and the Mimosa: Knut Hamsun's Portrayal of the Inspired Artist." *Germanic Notes and Reviews* 40, no. 1 (2009): 10-21.

Buttry, Dolores. "Pursuit and Confrontation: The Short Stories of Knut Hamsun." *Scandinavian Studies* 70, no. 2 (1998): 233-250.

Buvik, Per. "Kunsten, Kjønnet, og Kvinnen om Ibsens Når Vi Døde Vågner," in *Livet på Likstrå: Henrik Ibsens Når Vi Døde Vågner.* Edited by Lisbeth P. Wærp, 179-210. Oslo: Landslaget for Norskundervisning og Cappelen Akademisk Forlag, 1999.

Caruth, Cathy. *Unclaimed Experience: Trauma, Narrative, and History.* Baltimore and London: John Hopkins University Press, 1996.

Cates, Caleb, Bruner, M. Lane, and Moss III, Joseph T. "Recuperating the Real: New Materialism, Object-Oriented Ontology, and Neo-Lacanian Ontical Cartography," *Philosophy & Rhetoric,* vol. 51, no. 2, 2018, pp. 151-175.

Columban, Alexandra. "Myths of Literary Creativity in Knut Hamsun's Hunger (1890) and Pan, from Lieutenant Thomas Glahn's Papers (1894)." *Philologia* 56, no. 3 (2011): 203-213.

Copjec, Joan. *Imagine There's No Woman.* Cambridge: MIT Press, 2004.

Davis, Colin. "État Présent: Hautology, Spectres and Phantoms." In *The Spectralities Reader: Ghosts and Haunting in Contemporary Cultural Theory,* edited by María del Pilar Blanco and Esther Peeren, 53-60. New York and London: Bloomsbury Academic, 2013.

Davis, Colin. *Haunted Subjects: Deconstruction, Psychoanalysis and the Return of the Dead.* New York: Palgrave Macmillan, 2007.

DeLong, Anne. *The Female Fantastic: Gendering the Supernatural in the 1890s and 1920s*. Edited by Lizzie Harris McCormick, Jennifer Mitchell, and Rebecca Soares 5-19. New York and London: Routledge, 2019.

Deleuze, Gilles. *Difference and Repetition.* Translated by Paul Patton. New York: Columbia University Press, 1994.

Derrida, Jacques. *Specters of Marx.* Translated by Peggy Kamuf. New York and London: Routledge, 1994.

Derrida, Jacques & Stiegler, Bernard. *The Spectralities Reader: Ghosts and Haunting in Contemporary Cultural Theory*. Edited by María del Pilar Blanco and Esther Peeren New York and London: Bloomsbury Academic, 2013.

Dolar, Mladen. "'I Shall Be with you on Your Wedding-Night': Lacan and the Uncanny," in *October* 58 (Autumn 1991): 5-23.

Elbek, Jørgen. "The Nordic Nineties." *Fin(s) de Siècle in Scandinavian perspective: Studies in Honor of Harald S. Naess.* Edited by Faith Ingwersen and Mary Kay Norseng, 55-68. Columbia: Camden House, 1993.

Evangelista, Stefano. "The Time of Ola Hansson: Translating Scandinavian Decadence in fin de siècle France and England," *Nordic Literature of Decadence.* Edited by Pirjo Lyytikäinen, Riikka Rossi, Viola Parente-Čapková, and Mirjam Hinrikus, 205-222. New York: Routledge, 2020.

Faivre, Antoine. *Western esotericism: a concise history*. New York: Suny Press, 2010.

Freud, Sigmund. *The Interpretation of Dreams*, Translated and Edited by James Strachey. New York: Basic Books, 2010.

Freud, Sigmund. "Medusa's Head," in *Writings on Art and Literature*, Edited by Werner Hamacher & David E. Wellbery, 264-265. Stanford: Stanford University Press, 1997.

Freud, Sigmund. "On Narcissism," in *The Freud Reader*, edited by Peter Gay, 545-561. New York: W.W. Norton & Co. Inc, 1989.

Freud, Sigmund. *Ego and the Id.* Edited by P. Gay. New York: W.W. Norton & Company Inc, 1960.

Freud, Sigmund. "The Uncanny," in *The Standard Edition of the Complete Psychological Works of Sigmund Freud*, Trans by James Strachey, Vol. XVII, 219-252. London: The Hogarth Press, 1925.

Foster, Hal. "Medusa and the Real," *RES: Anthropology and Aesthetics*, No. 44, (August 2003): 181-190.

Fuchs, Elinor. "The Apocalyptic Ibsen: When We Dead Awaken." *Twentieth Century Literature* 46, no. 4 (2000): 396-404.

Germes, Ken. 2009. "Freud and Nietzsche on Sublimation." *Journal of Nietzsche Studies* 39, no. Fall (2009): 38-59.

Gordon, Avery F. *Ghostly Matters: Haunting and the Sociological Imagination*. Minneapolis: University of Minnesota Press, 2008.

Hamsun, Knut. "Unconscious Life of the Mind," in *Acta Nordica Studier i språk- og litteraturevitenskap*. Edited by Ståle Dingstad, Ylva Frød, Elisabeth Oxfeldt, and Ellen Rees, 281-289. Cambridge: Tapic Academic Press, 2011.

Hamsun, Knut. *Knut Hamsun: Selected Letters Volume I 1879-1898*. Translated by Harold Næss & James McFarlane, Oslo: Norvik Press, 1990.

Hamsun, Knut. *Pan: Av Løitnant Thomas Glahns Papirer*. Oslo: Glydendal Norsk Forlag, 1968.

Hamsun, Knut. *Victoria*. Oslo: Gyldendal Norsk Forlag, 1964.

Hamsun, Knut. *Mysterier*. Oslo: Gyldendal Norsk Forlag, 1954.

Hamsun. Knut. "Dronningen av Saba," In *Samlede romancer og fortællinger*, 7-28. Kristiania og Køvenhavn: Gyldendalske Boghandel Nordisk Forlag, 1908.
Hamsun, Knut. *Munken Vendt*. København: Gyldendalske Boghandel Nordisk Forlag (F. Hegel & Søn), 1902.

Hansson, Ola. *Sensitiva Amorosa*. Translated by Paul Norlen. Wisconsin: Department of Scandinavian Studies University of Wisconsin, 2002.

Helland, Frode. "Irene: Objekt eller Subjekt?" in *Livet på Likstrå: Henrik Ibsens Når Vi Døde Vågner*. Edited by Lisbeth P. Wærp, 125-148. Oslo: Landslaget for Norskundervisning og Cappelen Akademisk Forlag, 1999.

Ibsen, Henrik. "Når Vi Døde Vågner" In *Samlede Værker, femte bind*, 363-411. Kristiania og Køvenhavn: Glydendalske Boghandel Nordisk Forlag, 1907.

Jagodzinski, Jan. “The Site/Cite of Jacques Lacan or Forget Slavoj Žižek? Implications for Art and Its Education.” *Visual Arts Research* 36, no. 2 (Winter 2010): 15-37.

Kittang, Atle. *Luft, Vind, Ingenging.* Oslo: Gyldendal Norsk Forlag, 1984.

Kolloen, Ingar Sletten. *Knut Hamsun: Dreamer and Dissenter.* Translated by Deborah Dawkin & Erik Skuggevik. New Haven: Yale University Press, 2009.

Krouk, Dean. “Prophet of Regeneration: On Two Fascist Readings of Knut Hamsun” in *Nordlit*, 25, Juni (2010): 29-40.

Kruszelnicki, Michal. “Thomas Glahn and Johan Nagel: Towards the Abyss of Life’s Tragic Indeterminacy,” *Nordlit* 13, no. 2 (2010): 123-146.

Lacan, Jacques. *Desire and Its Interpretations.* Translated by Cormac Gallagher. www.lacaninireland.com, 2018.

Lacan, Jacques. “Field and Function of Speech and Language in Psychoanalysis,” In *Ecrits.* Translated by Bruce Fink, 197-268. New York and London: W.W. Norton & Company Inc, 2006.

Lacan, Jacques. “Seminar on ‘The Purloined Letter’” In *Ecrits.* Translated by Bruce Fink, 6-48. New York and London: W.W. Norton & Company Inc, 2006.

Lacan, Jacques. *The Four Fundamental Concepts of Psychoanalysis.* Translated by Alan Sheridan. New York and London: W.W. Norton & Company, Inc, 1998.

Lacan, Jacques. *Freud’s Papers on Technique 1953-1954.* Translated by John Forrester. New York and London: W.W. Norton & Company, Inc, 1991.

Lacan, Jacques. *The Ethics of Psychoanalysis 1959-1960.* Translated by Dennis Porter. New York and London: W.W. Norton & Company, Inc, 1986.

Loewald, Hans W. *Sublimation: Inquiries into Theoretical Psychoanalysis.* New Haven: Yale University Press, 1988.

Lunde, Arne. “Politics, Aesthetics, and Afterlife in På gjengrodde stier: Retracing Knut Hamsun’s ‘Overgrown Paths’ Toward Nazism.” In *Scandinaviaca* 47, no. 2 (2008): 175-90.

Lyytikäinen, Pirjo, Rossi Riikka, Parente-Čapková, Viola, Hinrikus, Mirjam. *Nordic Literature of Decadence.* New York and Milton Park: Routledge, 2020.

McFarlane, J.W. "The Whisper of the Blood: A Study of Knut Hamsun's Early Novels." *Modern Language Association* 71, no. 4 (1956): 563-594.

Miller, Arthur A. "An Interpretation of the Symbolism of Medusa." *American Imago* 15, no. 4 (Winter 1958): 389-399.

Næss, Harald. "George Brandes and 19th Century Scandinavian Realism." *Neohelicon* 15, no. 2 (1988): 114-134.

Nærup, Carl. *Illustretet Norsk Litteraturshistorie*. Kristiania: Det Norske Akiteforlang, 1905.

Norseng, Mary Kay. *Sigbjørn Obstfelder*. Boston: Twayne Publishers, 1982.

Obstfelder, Sigbjørn. "Korset," *Skrifter II*, 55-132. København: Glydendalske Boghandels Forlag, 1907.

Oxfeldt, Elisabeth. *Nordic Orientalism: Paris and the Cosmopolitan Imagination 1800-1900*. Copenhagen: Museum Tusculanum Press University of Copenhagen, 2005.

Oxfeldt, Elisabeth. "Orientalism, Decadence and Ekphrasis in Hamsun's 'Dronningen av Saba,'" *Edda* 2 (2003): 181-194.

Proust, Marcel. *In Search of Lost Time: Swann's Way*, Translated by C.K. Scott Moncrieff and Terence Kilmartin. New York: The Modern Library, 2003.

Rees, Ellen. "Over-Determined Topography in Knut Hamsun's 'Dronningen Av Saba.'" *Scandinavian Studies* 80, no. 2 (2008): 185–200.

Reinert, Otto. "Ibsen and Mimesis." *Scandinavian Studies* 82, no. 2 (Summer 2010): 213-230.

Rossel, Sven. H. *A History of Scandinavian Literature, 1870-1980*. Translated by Anne C. Ulmer. Minneapolis: University of Minnesota Press, 1982.

Sjåvik, Jan. "Triangular Structures in Knut Hamsun's 'Pan." *Pacific Coast Philology* 27, no.1/2, (1992):117-123.

Spoo, Robert. "Uncanny Returns in 'The Dead': Ibsenian Intertexts and the Estranged Infant." In *Joyce: The Return of the Repressed*, edited by Susan Stanford Friedman, 89-113. Cornell University Press, 1993.

Todorov, Tzvetan. *The Fantastic: A Structural Approach to a Literary Genre*. Translated by

Richard Howard. Cleveland/London: The Press of Case Western Reserve University, 1973.

Von Shnurbein, Stefanie. "Knut Hamsun's Narrative Fetishism," in *Acta Nordica Studier i språk-og litteraturevitenskap*. Edited by Ståle Dingstad, Ylva Frød, Elisabeth Oxfeldt, and Ellen Rees, 47-64. Tapic Academic Press, 2011.

Wærp, Henning Howlid . "Knut Hamsun's *Pan*: Nordlandsnatur eller symbollandskap?" in Hele Livet en Vandrer i Nature: Økokristiske Lesninger i Knut Hamsuns Forfatterskap,116-135. Stamsund: Orkana Akademisk, 2018.

Weinstock, Jeffrey Andrew. "from Introduction: The Spectral Turn." *The Spectralities Reader: Ghosts and Haunting in Contemporary Cultural Theory*. Edited by María del Pilar Blanco and Esther Peeren, 61-68. New York and London: Bloomsbury Academic, 2013.

Wicklund, Beret. "Kjønnskampens Kunst, Kunsten som Kjønnskamp," in *Livet på Likstrå: Henrik Ibsens Når Vi Døde Vågner*. Edited by Lisbeth P. Wærp, 202-228. Oslo: Landslaget for Norskundervisning og Cappelen Akademisk Forlag, 1999.

Wiehr, Josef. *Knut Hamsun: His Personality and His Outlook upon Life*. Northampton and Paris: Smith College Studies in Modern Languages, 1922.

Žagar, Monika. *The Dark Side of Literary Brilliance*. Seattle: University of Washington Press, 2009.

Zupančič, Alenka. "On Love as Comedy," *Journal for Politics, Gender and Culture* 2, no. 2 (Summer 2003): 61-80.

Index

V

W

Z

www.ingramcontent.com/pod-product-compliance
Lightning Source LLC
LaVergne TN
LVHW010719210926
848485LV00008B/1459/J
9781680535730